Hey, children on th spectrum can play too!

This book has been written to support those working or living with children on the autism spectrum. Author Wendy Usher uses over 30 years of experience, both as a parent of a young woman with Aspergers Syndrome and as a professional. The book brings insights and ideas in an easy to understand and practical way.

The various case studies and stories are true; however names and details have been changed to protect the identities of the children and families concerned.

This book is one of a series published by The Play Doctors supporting inclusion. Each book provides thoughts and resources to help adults work with all children to ensure they are offered the same chances and experiences as others.

"We recognise that play is a continuum, fundamental to all stages of life and takes many different forms.
The values and benefits of the play experience we have as children help mould us into adulthood and as adults we each have a responsibility to empower children to play freely and in turn grow old having lived a life using the skills and knowledge gained from the play we encourage today! "

Wendy Usher

All rights reserved. No part of this publication may be reproduced or transmitted in any form or by any means, electronically or mechanically, including photocopying, recording or any information storage or retrieval system, without either prior permission in writing from the publisher The Play Doctors Ltd

All photographs in this book are accredited to iStockphoto.com or produced with written permission of the parents and/or guardians of the children discussed and of the children themselves. The names of both adults and the children have been changed to protect their privacy.

Second Edition first published 2010
Published by The Play Doctors Ltd 2011
© Wendy Usher
ISBN Number: 97- 0-9566690-0-1

Content

Chapter One: Dealing with expectations

Throughout our lives we have expectations of how people will respond and react based on our own experiences and understanding of the world around us. We make sense of the world by experimenting and seeing what happens; we learn by the result, and remember for the next time we face a similar experience, adapting our learning accordingly.

The knowledge we gain provides us with a sense of anticipation and expectation of how others will respond to situations. If that expectation is not met then we hesitate, not always knowing how to react.

Some responses we have are inbuilt and we do them without thinking or necessarily being aware of what we are doing. These are spontaneous actions such as smiling, laughing or jumping at the unexpected.

Others are based on curiosity and observation such as a toddler who has just learnt to walk, who stops to pick up stones or leaves.

We gain a level of understanding that helps support us as we grow into adulthood. Through this understanding we have an expectation and assumption of how others, children and adults, will respond and behave.

Children on the autism spectrum may not react, respond or behave in the way we expect and may not see the world in the same way that we do.

We are all different, with individual likes and dislikes, and with different ways of thinking and processing information. Children on the autism spectrum are individuals too, who just happen to have autism.

If a young baby cries we recognise that they may be hungry, thirsty, need changing, are tired, in pain or just want human contact and cuddles. We respond accordingly, even though the baby is unable to tell us exactly what they are crying for. We experiment until we get it right, adapting our responses until we get a favourable result.

As the child grows, so do our expectations of them. We expect that they will be able to tell us what is wrong, explain their likes and dislikes and that they will begin to make their own choices and decisions based on this development.

Every child is different, and we appreciate they may have particular preferences. For instance, some people enjoy physical contact and will want to touch; for others this is uncomfortable and they would prefer to only be touched by immediate members of their family. We change our responses according to who we are with.

It is not always easy for someone on the autism spectrum to 'read others' and to recognise the type of response they may get to their actions. We also may find it hard to read the mind of someone on the autism spectrum.

Our expectations are based on life experiences which influence our own response to others; we may become fearful or anxious when the reaction is not what we anticipate. We can either adapt our own approach and expectation, accepting the other person's response, or we try to coerce them into conforming, encouraging the type of the response we expect to see.

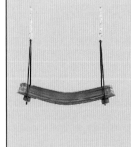
Catherine, who is on the autism spectrum, was playing in the park with her friend Sam. While they were swinging, Sam fell off the swing and grazed her knees. While she was still lying on the ground crying and upset Catherine made an observation. "You know," she said, "when you fell off the swing, it went faster without you on it."

There was no empathy for Sam; Catherine did not respond to the incident in the way that would have been expected, she did not go to help her friend or offer sympathy. She was more interested in the dynamics of the swing.

There are many kinds of impairments, seen and unseen. If we are working with someone who has a physical impairment we can appreciate the kinds of adaptations that may be necessary to ensure they are included in activities.

Autism is known as one of the unseen disabilities. Adaptations that are required to ensure that children and young people are included are not as easy to assess. This book will help you to think creatively and 'outside the box' to adapt the way we work and the environment in order to support children's access of play and free time activities.

There are two models of disability: the social model and the medical model. The medical model assumes that the disabled person is the problem; it is because of their specific impairment that they cannot join in. The social model takes a different view, recognising that, if society adapted, disabled people could access the activity. This book looks at how to support children using the social model.

When working with children on the autism spectrum this may mean: making changes to the physical environment; adapting the way you communicate; adapting play activities to include special interests; and, most of all, adapting our expectations and being flexible to recognise individual requirements.

No two children on the autism spectrum will be the same; each will respond differently. What works well for some will not work in the same way for others. The most important role you have is to get to know your children well, understand their individuality and respond accordingly.

Christopher likes bright colours. His room is painted blue and white, the colours of his favourite football team. He has scarves and ribbons hung up and the walls are covered in posters. He enjoys being surrounded by colours.

Christopher finds it difficult to deal with sensory overload. When there is too much going on he needs time out to calm down. This relates to all senses including visual stimulation. On occasion, he would try to attack a play worker for no reason. After observation, it was discovered that he only ever attacked her when she was wearing a bright red fleece. He has a particular aversion to the colour red.

The social and medical models of disability

The medical model of disability sees the child as:
- **Incapable**
- **Having an illness**
- **Requiring special provision**
- **In need of therapy**
- **Autistic**

The problem with this model is that the condition or impairment is central. The child is powerless; decisions are made on their behalf with little or no consultation. The child is seen as ill and in need of treatment, and the emphasis is placed on a cure. The child is coerced into a behaviour framework that is alien to them and therefore finds it very difficult to adapt.

The social model of disability recognises:
- **The child just happens to have autism**
- **Adaptations will be made to ensure his individual requirements are met and that he is included**
- **Through this approach, the child will be given choices and will be able to control his play**

The social model puts the individual firmly in the centre; someone who just happens to have a disability but that is secondary. The individual is the more important.

There is an expectation that play workers will adapt the environment and, if necessary, the way they interact with the individual using appropriate communication strategies and techniques. The child is able to be him/herself, supported by play workers who adapt the setting rather than expect the child to adapt.

Identifying barriers to play

Before we start to unpack the traits of autism, it is important to recognise the barriers to participation that some children face. This book will support your understanding of the triad of impairment and will provide examples of how play has been adapted through short stories and case studies.

To provide good play opportunities for all children we need to appreciate all barriers, not just to the child but to their family and the play settings themselves.

The voice of children and young people

We asked a group of children on the autism spectrum what they felt stopped them playing. Responses included:

- Mum won't let me
- The staff don't understand me
- They don't do what I like doing
- I never know what is going to happen next; I need to know what is happening all the time
- There are too many other children
- The workers shout and I don't like it
- I don't get invited to play, I just watch the others

The voice of play settings

We approached adults responsible for planning play (including lunchtime supervisors), who recognised some barriers to participation, including:

- General lack of understanding leading to fear of the unknown
- Lack of knowledge relating to specific augmented communication systems used
- Adults did not always know how to react to children's lack of social engagement or lack of understanding of the unspoken social rules
- Some staff lacked the ability to 'read ahead' of a situation and to put appropriate measures into place to support children
- Staff did not know how to 'draw a child into play' when they seem withdrawn or fixated on specific play or obsessional behaviour
- Staff were confused in knowing how to manage behaviour traits

The voice of the parents

We approached parents directly and asked them what their concerns were in allowing their children on the autism spectrum to play. They included:

- Not allowing a child to attend a play setting because they do not know if the staff have experience or training
- Not knowing if the play setting is physically safe (boundaries/fences)
- Some parents believe staff have a fear of disability, i.e. 'rabbit in the headlights' approach, which needs to be eliminated
- Staff need to sometimes think 'outside the box' to create different approaches for different children
- Parents wanted settings to have a point of contact to talk about any specific issues. It was a barrier not knowing who to talk to
- Families felt rigid rules were a barrier and wanted a flexible approach, for example, allowing a disabled 9-year-old child to join in with the 5-8 yrs group as the disabled child would feel more comfortable with this group
- Large groups and lots of noise are not always suitable for disabled children
- Activity schemes should adapt the signing in process to be inclusive for disabled children. Some children find it difficult to queue and be around lots of people and noise. For some parents this was a barrier to participation. Children found it so difficult to queue the parents did not return
- Registration forms should have an 'all about me' space so parents can fill out a profile of how their child may present the triad of impairment rather than a small tick box section to write in medication and doctor's information
- Parents find the exclusion of their children on the basis of behaviour very offensive, almost like saying to a child: "If you can't get out of your wheelchair and walk you can't come in" (medical model of disability)
- Parents find there is sometimes an element of danger for their child when placed in an open access setting. Therefore, parents ask that the workers give clear boundaries to all children, and for those boundaries to be reiterated each session
- Parents want an opportunity to meet the staff or have a free taster session for the children to see if they like it, in order to alleviate fears and reduce barriers to participation

The bullet points above were provided directly by parents, play staff and disabled children. It is essential that their voices are heard.

Chapter Two:
A bit about autism

The term 'autism' has different meanings for different people depending on their own experience or based on what they may have read in the media.

Autism is just one of several names that may be used to describe a developmental condition affecting the way a person thinks and communicates with others and the world around them.

The condition is described as an autism spectrum disorder, sometimes known as ASD or ASC (autism spectrum condition). This means that people may have impairments to a greater or lesser extent in three primary areas. There are a number of associated conditions known as social communication disorders or impairments which have similar traits. In this book we will refer to the autism spectrum as ASC.

The spectrum referred to identifies how groups of people diagnosed with ASC may present. Some may have classic autism and are known as 'low functioning', unable to live independently without support. Others have traits of autism known as 'high functioning' and may live independently or may require some level of support; this condition is generally known as Aspergers Syndrome. There are many individuals who have traits of autism but have never been assessed or formally diagnosed.

As you read through this resource book you may recognise traits of autism in yourself, friends and family. It is said that we all have traits to some extent.

The way in which autism presents can vary depending on the individual. We are all individuals first, with different likes and dislikes, interests and anxieties. People on the autism spectrum may have certain behaviours and traits that are typical of the condition.

We all get stressed at some point in the day and, when we do, we become less rational and logical. People on the autism spectrum are no different; they can also be relaxed or get stressed. Sometimes this can cause them to slide slightly up and down the spectrum, on some days displaying more autistic traits than on others.

A bit of background: the term 'autism' has been around for more than one hundred years. The word comes from the Greek 'autos' meaning 'self'. A description of a person isolated from the world; an 'isolated self'. Various doctors researched the condition and, prior to the 1960s, linked autism to schizophrenia. This is now known to be a separate condition, although there are close parallels in how they can present.

Back in the 1940s, the term 'autism' was used to describe children with emotional or social problems. Dr. Leo Kanner undertook a study with a number of children and used the term to describe the withdrawn behaviour he observed. At the same time, a German scientist, Hans Asperger, worked with a group of older children and recorded a range of traits where children had similar impairments but to a lesser extent. This condition was named after him and is now known as Aspergers Syndrome.

Jamie, a young man on the autism spectrum, was in court as a witness. During the trial he remonstrated with the judge for pronouncing Aspergers as in 'mergers' rather that Aspergers as in 'beef burgers'.

To him at the time, the pronunciation of Aspergers was more important than the evidence he was giving and he had to let the judge know he was wrong, regardless of where he was or what he was doing.

Often, people on the higher functioning end of the spectrum are very pedantic, particularly in their speech, and have no fear of telling others if they have got it wrong. If unsure ask the individual how they would like to pronounce words.

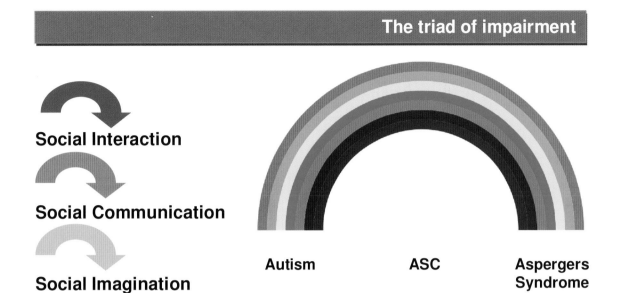

Social Interaction

Social Communication

Social Imagination

Autism   ASC   Aspergers Syndrome

The spectrum refers to people who experience traits of autism in three distinct areas: socialisation, communication and imagination.

Let's give this some context. The spectrum is often described as a rainbow with three different colours, each colour representing one area of impairment. To the left of the spectrum we have placed classic autism, and to the right, Aspergers Syndrome.

The three areas are often referred to as the 'triad of impairment'. This term was coined through the work of Lorna Wing and Judith Gould in 1979. A study was undertaken of 132 children, who attended special schools in Camberwell, London. Each of these children presented with one or more traits within the triad.

The group was divided, based on their social behaviour, with 58 children showing appropriate social interaction and 74 showing a social impairment to a greater or lesser degree. The research concluded:

"All the children with social impairments had repetitive stereotyped behaviour and almost all had absence or abnormalities of language and symbolic activities. Thus the study showed a marked tendency for these problems to occur together."

The research also identified that there were more boys than girls who exhibited these traits. It is now thought that there are 4 males to every 1 female diagnosed with ASC.

The triad of impairment can be described or visualised in many ways; sometimes it is illustrated as a circle or triangle.

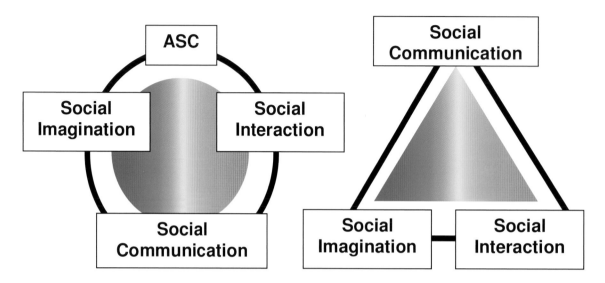

All children on the autism spectrum will have difficulties in these three areas. However, as always, things are not as simple as they seem, as there are a number of other traits associated to autism that are not within the triad. Some (not all) children may have sensory sensitivities where they are over or under sensitive to stimuli. As in the previous example, some children may be particularly sensitive to the colour red, finding it very arousing and creating the emotion of anger. Some children may have a very low (or high) pain threshold and be over or under sensitive to pain; others will hate the feel of water or sensory stimuli.

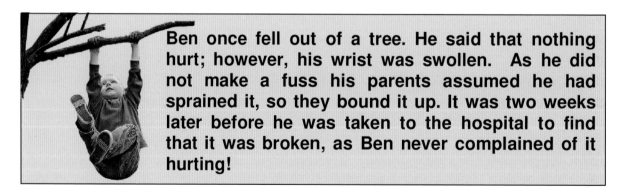

Ben once fell out of a tree. He said that nothing hurt; however, his wrist was swollen. As he did not make a fuss his parents assumed he had sprained it, so they bound it up. It was two weeks later before he was taken to the hospital to find that it was broken, as Ben never complained of it hurting!

Individuals on the autism spectrum may have particular interests and obsessions, types of mannerisms or repetitive movements such as flapping hands or turning in a tight circle. Some children may have echolalia, copying others' speech, language or behaviour. These are explored in more detail later in the book.

10

The next few chapters begin to describe how the triad of impairment presents through a series of case studies and stories following a group of four children and young people, focusing on play and free-time activities.

The case studies look at different times in their lives and describe various aspects of their personal stories. Additional short stories about other children or young people illustrate other aspects of how autism may present.

Christopher   **Joseph (Joe)**   **Catherine**   **Suminda**

We also refer to Mary, who was diagnosed with Aspergers Syndrome when she was 14, and is now an adult.

We will look at how to support children on the spectrum, describe what worked well and why, and what did not work well. The book aims to increase your understanding and awareness of ASC and to help you to identify strategies and techniques that you can use on a daily basis to support children and young people to join in, have fun and play!

There is no 'one stop shop' or 'cure all'. The ideas in this book are those that have been tried and tested over time. What works well on one day may not work on the next, and you will have to rethink. The book aims to open your mind and encourages you to think 'out of the box'.

Not all children portray the triad of impairment in the same way. Each child or young person is individual and has their own personalities; however, there are some similar traits that will be found. The chart below indicates where the traits of autism fall on the spectrum for each of the individual children.

 Christopher is represented by a triangle

He has poor social interaction and no speech but does use some augmented communication and has very little imagination.

 Joe is represented by a circle

He has fairly good social interaction, but misunderstands others' intentions and does not understand unspoken social rules. He tends to talk 'at you' rather than with you and has very literal thinking.

 Catherine is represented by a diamond

She worries about social interaction and finds it difficult as she does not know how to respond to others. Her communication is good. However, she prefers to let others talk but will communicate well when necessary. Catherine has little imagination and takes things literally.

 Suminda is represented by a star

She is a very sociable girl, enjoying others' company but she does not always understand when others have 'had enough'. She uses augmented communication systems including signing and the use of symbol cards. Her imagination is quite poor and she lacks the skill to play creatively.

 Mary is represented by a square

She is very sociable, enjoying older people's company. She has good verbal communication but does not understand nuances or facial expressions. She lacks imagination. However, she copies others' behaviour or displays learnt behaviour.

Where the children fall on the autism spectrum

Social Interaction	△	◇ ○	☆ ■
Social Communication	△ ☆		○ ◇ ■
Social Imagination	△	☆ ◇ ○	■

Autism ⟷ **Aspergers**

Chapter Three:
The triad of impairment uncovered

Each of the areas described within the triad is intrinsically linked. The colours of the rainbow may blend. When we begin to describe how children on the spectrum may socialise, the case study or story may also reflect how this impacts on the child's ability to communicate or think creatively and imaginatively.

However, we will begin at the beginning and initially look at how each area of impairment may present generally before moving on to individual stories.

Social Interaction

Many people on the spectrum find it difficult to socialise with others and engage in the unspoken social rules, for instance, appreciating personal space or understanding how friendships are built.

As social situations may sometimes be uncomfortable, people on the spectrum may avoid contact with others and may not understand when, where or how to be sociable.

Each individual interacts socially in different ways. Here we have identified three distinct groups. The majority of individuals on the autism spectrum fall into one of these groups.

However, remember that each person is individual and there are always exceptions to the rule!

The aloof group

In this group, children are often referred to as 'being in a world of their own'. Children may not necessarily see others as individuals. They may behave as though others do not exist or are inanimate objects. Little or no eye contact is made and there is a lack of response when being spoken to by others.

Often, faces have little or no expression; it is very difficult to know what a child on the autism spectrum is thinking or feeling. Very few visual cues are given out by the individual unless the emotion is extreme: anger, distress, happiness or joy.

Children may not respond to other people's emotions, for instance, a lack of interest and response to being cuddled or praised. Some children will prefer to play on their own with a very limited repertoire of self-directed play. Self-chosen activities may be limited to lining up cars or constantly watching the same DVD. Some children do, however, enjoy rough and tumble play, laughing and giggling, but when the play stops the aloofness returns. Some children may display unusual behaviours such as flapping, spinning, making noises, giggling or laughing inappropriately.

Consider this: If you needed to undo an electric plug to change a fuse what tool would you need for the job?

A screwdriver!

You would fetch the tool, undo the screw and change the fuse. The screwdriver is an inanimate object; it does not require you to ask if it is feeling alright, if you were happy with the way it undid the screw and it does not require you to say thank you.

Some children on the spectrum will use adults or other children as a tool, a 'means to an end' rather than interact and socialise with them when asking for help.

Christopher does not interact with others on a social basis. He walks through other groups of children as if they were not there. He will interact when he wants something or needs help. However, there are no smiles or verbal communication.

When Christopher wants to play with play dough, but cannot get the lid off the pot, he looks around for a tool to do the job. The tool is an adult's hand, so, going over to the adult, he takes hold of the tool and brings it back to the play dough pot.

No social interaction or engagement occurs from Christopher during this exchange.

The adult needs to interact with Christopher and encourage him to participate in a form of communication. The play worker should talk to him and may use a symbol card or signing to encourage a response.

The passive group

In this group, children may have eye contact and accept social approaches. They may want to join in but not always understand the social rules of the game such as turn taking and sharing.

As children get older, they may wish to have friends and build relationships but find this hard to do. Some children will instigate games and activities, but on their terms. They will talk 'at' you rather than 'with' you, and assume that you are as interested in their hobbies as they are. Children will generally respond to directness, if adults say: "Stop talking about your hobby now" they will stop. Nuances and hints will not work. Be direct.

Children may not see the world in the same way as we do and will relate to the world differently. Some children may have particular behavioural traits that are seen as unsocial, for instance, smelling others, feeling others, shouting loudly or making noises.

Joe attends a mainstream school. He is in a class that is highly structured with clear boundaries. When he knows what he should be doing he gets on with the job quickly and well.

Joe was diagnosed with Aspergers Syndrome when he was 8 years old; he is now 10. Joe enjoys being in the company of other children. He sometimes has difficulty in building and maintaining social relationships.

At school, Joe was asked to play in a game of football. He was given the job of goalie and was told if the ball came near to him he was to pick it up and throw it back.

During the game, the ball was kicked at Joe's goal. He caught the ball and his team cheered. Joe was thrilled; he knew the others were pleased with him.

At that point, the players started to call out: "Over here, Joe! Chuck it over here!"

Unfortunately, one of the opposing team called out the same thing. Joe did what he had been asked: he threw the ball to the player who had asked for it.

Joe's team was really cross with him, but he had no idea why. All he had done was to do what had been asked of him. Joe did not understand the 'rules of the game'.

The coach explained to Joe the rules of the game and got him to apologise to his team. Joe still did not really understand what he had done wrong. We need to consider the experience from the viewpoint of the person on the spectrum. Be clear and concise with explanation, be honest and help the individual to learn from mistakes. Explain what went wrong, and why, and what else could have happened.

Acting differently
(outside of the social norm)

Here, a child or young person may be seen as 'the odd one out'. Have you ever observed a child in the school playground who is hanging back and not joining in with others, the one who needs encouragement and support to meet and make new friends?

These young people may display learnt or copied behaviour, speech, mannerisms and responses. This is known as 'echolalia' and is explored further later in the book.

Individuals may not understand the social rules and hug the wrong person or may not display warmth at all, instead, shaking hands formally with parents and relatives.

Language use may be excellent, but very exact, as though learned from a dictionary rather than socially. Some language may be stilted or formal and used in a very literal sense.

Some children or young people may make active approaches to others, but make contact in different or seemingly strange ways. Attention may not be paid to the person speaking, eye contact may be nonexistent or too intense and personal space may be invaded.

As the child grows to become an adult, they may become excessively polite and formal, trying hard to stay within the rules for social engagement, but not really understanding them.

Mary, now an adult, works in a residential care home. One day she went to the pub with her work colleagues where she was told a particularly rude joke. At the pub everyone laughed.

She was surprised later that day when Matron and Masie (an 89-year-old resident) did not find the joke funny. Mary had no understanding of what is socially acceptable in a given situation.

In this instance, Mary needs to be told what is socially acceptable or the same situation will occur again.

When Mary was 15, she was able to get her first job working part time in a local village supermarket. She was excited and looking forward to working.

Mary would regularly find herself in trouble. If the shop was busy she would be asked to stop loading shelves and instead work on the tills. She would happily transfer over to the tills but, without instruction, she would not then return to load shelves unless told to do so, even if there was no one waiting to be served.

The other staff would joke, often at her expense, because she was seen to be different. Mary would not understand the jokes but would realise that she was being teased, and did not like it, but could not explain why.

One evening, when her mum came to fetch her home, she found Mary crying. It was very unusual for her to show emotions. Instead of going home, her mum took her to the local garage that had a coffee bar. They sat having a cup of coffee and Mary's mum said to her: "I know it is difficult for you to describe, but unless you tell me what has upset you I cannot do anything to help." Mary's response was:

"If everyone in the world was a sheep, they would all be white sheep.
I am a black sheep and I want to be a white sheep.
I do not want to be different!"

As children on the autism spectrum grow and become adult, especially those who are at the more able end of the spectrum, they become more socially aware and recognise that they are different and may resent it. There are instances of young people becoming depressed and anxious. With support and advice there are lots of ways to help individuals and they will go on to lead fulfilling lives. However, they may need a little help on the way. Don't be frightened at speaking directly; it helps. Giving advice by insinuating is not always understood.

Within play, the adult's role is essential to support children and young people to feel included and wanted, reduce isolation and encourage friendships. Look for children with similar interests; create projects where children work together to achieve an end result.

During the school day, Catherine feels safe. She has a learning support assistant who helps, and she prefers the company of adults.

During play times and after school, she feels threatened as she is bullied by a group of girls who have found her to be an easy target. They have asked her for money, which she has given them, stealing it from her mother's purse.

On a school trip the children pair off into natural groups leaving Catherine on her own. The only children offering to go with her are the bullies. Catherine has a difficult choice but does not want to be on her own, so she agrees. During the trip, these children say that if she goes into a shop and steals two key rings for them, they will be her friend. She knows that this is not right. However, she does what the girls have asked.

She gets caught and ends up accused of shoplifting and is taken to the local police station. The school phone her mum to come and speak to the police...

We will come back to Catherine's story later in the book. However, the story so far illustrates the fact that some children may be vulnerable and need to be given skills to support their understanding of others' intentions.

Be aware of potential bullying in play settings, be vigilant and make time to listen to fears and worries.

Children who get on well with their play worker and enjoy play may relax, build relations and feel able to disclose and confide in them with their problems and concerns. Make time to chat, be available and open, willing to listen and be observant. We advocate making time to walk and talk!

Joe would come into the after school club in a very cross mood. It was difficult for the play workers to establish what the problem was and if they could help.

The setting used two boxes, one with a lid and the other without. These were Joe's boxes. When he came to the play setting he was able to draw, write or make a model about what was bothering him. If it was something that someone could help him with he put it in the open box and if it was something that was private he would put it in the closed box.

His personal assistant at the after school club would ask him if he wanted to share anything in the open box. Through this method, Joe disclosed that he was being bullied and needed help to know how to handle the bullies.

All children need support in knowing how to deal with bullies. However, children on the autism spectrum may need additional support and be given specific strategies. If the adult just stops the bullying occurring, the child has nothing to fall back on if it happens again when the adult is not there.

Some children may exhibit behaviours that are socially unacceptable, for instance, a young gentleman had learnt the joys of masturbation; unfortunately, in the middle of a supermarket was not an appropriate place. This young man needed to have clear boundaries as to where and when it was acceptable for him to participate in this activity.

Other children may display characteristics of autism that are seen as challenging but are not dangerous such as flapping and spinning. Ask yourself the reason behind the behaviour. Is the message: 'This situation scares me, I want to get out of here', or: 'I don't understand what's going to happen next'? Sometimes, specific behaviours are a comfort mechanism for individuals; something that is familiar and distracts them from whatever they are finding difficult.

Before stopping a particular behaviour, ask yourself why you are stopping it. Is it just embarrassing, dangerous or are you trying to teach a child what is socially acceptable? If so, have you suggested an alternative acceptable behaviour?

Many children wish to socialise but lack the skills to enable social relationships to develop and continue successfully. Encourage a range of social activities and games that include the need to communicate. Games like 'Happy Families' or 'tag' both involve the need to work together to achieve the final result.

Cambridge University ran a study inviting children with higher functioning autism (Aspergers Syndrome) to a Lego Club. The children had to abide by a set of simple, positive rules and worked in pairs or threes.

One child acted as the 'engineer' and described the instructions; another as the 'supplier', finding the correct pieces, and the 'builder' put the pieces together.

After a time, they would swap roles and later play 'freestyle' in pairs allowing them to practise compromise, think creatively and take others' ideas into account. The study helped many children to gain a social understanding, make friends and generate their own ideas through imaginative play.

Some children will not see the point in playing imaginatively; it has no meaning to them. The type of play described above is semi structured, allowing flexible thinking and creativity with an end result.

If you are meeting a child for the first time, try to find out a little about them and what they enjoy. Gather items that will be of relevance and show them that you are interested. Be aware of responses to physical touch. Some children may dislike touch. Check with the child's parents/guardians.

Reinforce positive actions by offering appropriate praise. Remember, social praise, such as words, may not be relevant. Consider using something more tangible, such as time to play with their favourite activity. Egg timers work well to indicate the passage of time.

Have some repetitive activities on hand; action games, songs and activities that involve social contact, and spend time with the children down on the floor. Don't be upset that you are not invited into play; the first step might be that you are accepted within their play space.

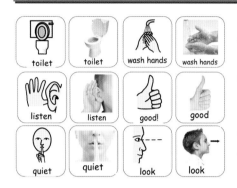

All children on the autism spectrum are individual and will favour a particular form of communication.

Some children find speech and language fascinating and will have a far greater vocabulary than many adults.

For others, auditory language is very difficult to process. Children may only respond to a few words within the sentence.

For some (20%), language is far too confusing; they prefer to stay silent and opt out of speech. This does not mean that they cannot speak in a physical sense. However, they choose not to speak and get their message across in other ways including behaviour.

Behaviour in itself is a form of communication.

If this is so, then what is the communication behind the behaviour?

Of course, communication is not all about speech and language. It is estimated that over 90% of our communication is via body language and unspoken signals. This includes: facial expression; showing emotion, pleasure and displeasure; giving encouraging signs; and exclusion and inclusion signs. It is very difficult for a child on the autism spectrum to read body language and interpret it clearly.

Research suggests this is why some children will not hold eye contact. The eyes are the 'window to the soul' and convey many messages. If these cannot be read, it is disconcerting and frightening for a child and therefore avoidance tactics are employed.

22

A famous university professor who was diagnosed with autism in 1950 is Dr. Temple Grandin. She is an animal scientist and has spent her life studying cows, and states that she enjoys their company more than humans.

Dr. Grandin is an inspiration to many, having written books and had a film made about her life. She didn't talk until she was three and a half years old, communicating her frustration instead by screaming, peeping and humming.

Despite the lack of verbal communication in her early years, she is now a renowned speaker and author and an inspiration to many.

Using speech

Let's break this down and clarify what areas of communication may be difficult for people on the autism spectrum.

The use of speech varies. Some children will have an excellent command of the spoken language and sound as though their speech has been learnt from a dictionary. They may well correct others if their speech and grammar is not correct.

Some children will give a far greater depth of explanation than necessary, particularly if the subject matter is of interest to them. They may not realise that you or others are bored.

Others find processing language very difficult and are unable to form their own sentences. These children may copy language; this is called echolalia, echoing the words of others. Echolalia may also refer to copied behaviour in addition to speech.

 **Ben was thirsty. He happened to be watching a television advertisement for Coca-Cola, which had the theme tune 'I'd like to teach the world to sing'. He equated the need for a drink with the theme tune.**

During a summer activity scheme Ben walked over to Cheryl, a play worker, and began to sing: "I'd like to teach the world to sing." His message was that he was thirsty and wanted a drink.

Cheryl did not understand this form of echolalic communication and joined in the song. After a while, she suggested that Ben went and sang this to another worker, Ben complied, but after 10 minutes was lying on the floor displaying a temper tantrum.

Ben's communication had not been understood. This form of echolalia is extreme. However, it provides an example that children may not only repeat others' words but may adopt a specific choice of words, song or sentence to express a need.

The play setting reported the incident to Mum. Her response was immediate: "Oh, Ben wanted a drink." However, this information about Ben's behaviour and form of communication had not been passed on to the setting.

It is very important to know and understand communication traits and individual requirements. Most play settings will ask the child or parent/guardian to complete an 'All about Me' form before attending sessions. Firstly, this should focus on the child: what do they like doing, what are their favourite activities, foods, drinks, colours, etc. Secondly, it is an opportunity to find out more about the child you are working with, including how they present traits within the autism spectrum, particularly in relation to communication and calming methods.

The concept of understanding 'me' or 'I' is difficult for some children. Suminda will not refer to herself as 'I' or 'me', but instead will say: "Suminda would like a drink", or will ask for things by repeating a phrase she associates with the action: "Do you want a drink?" meaning 'I want a drink'.

Some children will miss out linking words, using the minimum of speech in a similar manner to texting. Words such as 'in', 'on', 'the', 'because', 'over' or 'under' may not be used. A child may say "Walk park", rather than "Let's walk to the park" or "Can we go to the park?"

Most signing and symbol systems use the key words and miss out on the linking words. It is essential to support the child by repeating the sentence or request using all appropriate words, but keeping the sentence short and to the point.

Repetitive questioning is often a trait of language use. The answer is known by the asker, but the repetition of the words is fascinating to the child in the same way that a child may like to repeat a play activity such as lining up cars. If the question is asked back to the child, the answer (using the same language and tone of voice as the responder) may be given accurately.

"What time is it?"
"10 o'clock."

"What time is it?"
"You know the time. I have just told you."

A delay of a few seconds and then
the child asks again:

"What time is it?"

If the question is asked back to the child, she may be able to process the information and provide you with a response: **"You tell me what the time is."** Response: **"10 o'clock."**

Children may use words in a very distinctive manner. The word used may relate to their particular personal understanding and may not be generic. For instance, a neighbour owns a dog. Whenever the family see the dog they say: "Oh look, it's the dog." Therefore, in the child's mind the words 'the dog' relate solely to the neighbour's dog and not to other animals.

Be aware of the child's use of language. If confused, check with the parents or guardian. If you are aware of these particular traits, share the information with other co-workers and volunteers.

Understanding speech

Most children on the spectrum will have difficulty understanding metaphorical language. Consider the following:

> 'It's raining cats and dogs'
> 'She bit his head off'
> 'Break a leg'
> 'I smell a rat'
> 'He has a good heart'
> 'The black sheep of the family'

Words can be taken very literally. Consider the words you are using, for example, the question: What would you do if you cut yourself? is phrased to ascertain whether the child knows to call an adult or fetch a plaster. The response given by one young man was: "Bleed." Accurate, yes, but a literal interpretation of the question!

Language can be very scary to a person on the autism spectrum. Some individuals need to work very hard to translate the meaning behind the words and require more time to process and make sense of the sounds.

The majority of individuals on the autism spectrum understand some speech even if they do not verbalise themselves. There are various levels of understanding; children will additionally look for clues to help identify the meaning behind the words.

> **During an assessment, the consultant asked Christopher to come and sit beside him. While doing so, he patted the cushion on the seat next to him. Christopher happily went and sat down. Turning to his mother, the consultant said: "He has a good level of verbal understanding."**
>
> **His mother sat down on another seat, patted the cushion beside her and said: "Christopher, bananas, gooseberries and mouthwash." Christopher obediently came over and sat down beside her.**
>
> **"Ah," said the consultant, "I see that the visual indicator has more power than words."**

We need to support children's understanding by using non-verbal communication in addition to verbal. Remember this in play: the child may not respond to an invitation to play verbally. However, if at the same time a visual clue is held up such as a jigsaw, building block or ball they may then recognise and associate the clue with the play, happily joining in.

If non-verbal communication systems are used they all require the users to verbalise as well, with the exception of British Sign Language (BSL), which is classed as a language in its own right.

Some children will get confused when words have more than one meaning. Sometimes, words sound the same but are spelt differently, or they are spelt the same and have different meanings.

Consider the following:
- People who come from Poland are **Polish**
- Let's use this cloth to **polish** the floor
- I lost a **minute** earring. It was very small
- It was a **minute** before I found it
- I need to **wind** the clock up
- The **wind** is strong today
- I need to **record** the title of this **record**
- I **write** this letter
- I need to turn **right**
- The **rite** of passage
- There is a **herd** of cows. I **heard** them **low** over the **low** wall
- Let's **meet** to buy some **meat**
- I **read** a **red** book

Just a few examples; the world is full of confusing language.

Earlier in the book, we mentioned Mary telling Matron and an elderly resident a risqué joke. This was because she did not understand that what was appropriate in one situation was not appropriate in a different situation. We also read that Mary did not understand the innuendo and 'joshing' of work colleagues. Be aware of your own speech and language use.

It is difficult for someone who takes words very literally to appreciate humour and 'get the joke'. It is also hard to appreciate sarcasm, what is real and what is not. What is the meaning behind the words?

Some children and young people may not understand intonation or voice control. They will shout loudly all the time, or whisper softly. It may be that voices sound mechanical, like a robot's voice box, or monotonous, with no variance to pitch or tone.

Enunciation of words may be very literal and overemphasised, each consonant being sounded individually. Other children may not be able to pronounce words clearly and may make up their own words instead.

Suminda has a fascination with *Thomas the Tank Engine*. She enjoys watching the DVDs and has many books and story CDs.

Her speech and language are good and she has a wide vocabulary. However, she speaks in the same Liverpudlian accent as the storyteller in the *Thomas* stories, even though her parents have strong Scottish accents.

On occasion, Suminda uses things that have been said in the *Thomas* films to emphasis a point, to communicate a need or to show pleasure and displeasure. For example, one of her favourite phrases is:

"And Thomas was very unhappy," meaning 'I'm not happy'.

Later in the book we think about how a particular interest or obsession such as *Thomas the Tank Engine* can be extended beyond watching a DVD, to encourage creative and imaginative play.

Be aware that some children may experience sensory overload. They are unable to 'unpack' what is most important. For instance, you may be talking to a child and expecting a response. The child's senses are being bombarded by a variety of sounds, light, heat, colour and movement, among others. The sound of your voice is just one in a series of sensory experiences and the child may not realise that it is the most important.

Have you ever been in a situation where you need to turn off a radio or the television to concentrate? We make choices and are able to 'tune out' unimportant sensory stimulation to concentrate on what we are doing. This can be difficult for children on the spectrum; we need to consider the whole environment before making a judgement that the child is just misbehaving and not listening.

Helpful hints using verbal communication

It's not only about how the children communicate; it's about how we use language and how children hear us.

Catherine once described hearing the human voice as an express train coming into the station. When the train was in the distance it was easy to distinguish the sound; when the train was passing through the station the sound distorted and became a 'white noise' before travelling on so that sound again became clear before receding altogether. She does not always get a clear message.

Some children may just hear the beginning or end of a sentence. If a child is only hearing the end of this sentence, what might they do? "Don't walk on the road." Of course, walk on the road. Instead, say: "Walk on the pavement." If the child is hearing and responding to the last part of the sentence they will at least be safe!

Some general rules to follow when communicating with people on the autism spectrum.

Firstly, slow down. Give the person time to process the information you have given them. Don't use words that are unnecessary or may cause confusion. Think about what you are saying and look for a way to support the instruction using non-verbal clues.

Remember, many children will not realise that you are talking to them. Start a dialogue with their name: "Joe, go and get your shoes on. It is time to play." Joe may not realise you mean him if you are talking to the whole class, for instance: "Class, time for break. Go and put your shoes on." Joe's name is not 'class', and he may not see himself as part of the whole.

> **Suminda was travelling in the car with her parents when a dog ran out in front of the car and her father had to undertake an emergency stop. "Oh, ****!" said her dad.**
> **Suminda was quiet, but when they got to the cinema she happily repeated her new word time and time again:**
> **"Oh, ****!" "Oh, ****!" "Oh, ****!"**

To summarise:
- Remember, behaviour is a form of communication, so what is the behaviour itself communicating?
- Know your children; communicate with parents and guardians
- Look for embedded meaning in echolalic speech or behaviour
- Remember, some children will refer to themselves in the third person
- Help children to create sentences by cueing them in: "I want..."
- When children keep asking the same questions, ask the question back
- Recognise that some children have distinctive speech and use of words
- Don't use sarcasm, and avoid metaphorical language
- Be aware of literal translation of words
- Give the child time to process the words. If repeating a request, repeat using the same words
- Keep sentences short and to the point
- Back up verbal communication with visual cues
- Be yourself, be humorous and joke, but be aware the child may not understand humour
- Be accepting of a child's mannerisms in speech
- Some children may need encouragement to be quiet. Do not raise your own voice when asking a child to be quiet. Use non-verbal communication to support understanding
- Be positive, not negative, in both language and attitude

Non-verbal communication

For many children on the spectrum, non-verbal communication is the way in which they make the most sense of the world around them.

We know that verbal communication may be difficult for some. Processing the spoken word is not necessarily easy. By using non-verbal communication we can support individual children to gain a better understanding of what is meant by the words we use.

We use non-verbal communication all the time without realising it. By holding up an empty cup we may be signalling: Do you want a cup of tea? By frowning we are signalling the fact we are cross or perhaps concentrating.

Some children will only require a simple clue, while others rely on non-verbal communication systems such as symbols and signs. Many children will not recognise or equate facial expressions with emotions.

Joe's mum was cross with him. In fact she was very cross. "Go and put your toys away!" she said. Joe looked up at his mum.

"Wow, Mum," he said, "I can see a number eleven!" looking at her frown. Joe was not reading the emotion attached to the expression; he looked at the expression as a picture, without being able to read the message.

This chapter explores how non-verbal communication can support all children on the spectrum; communication generated by the speaker and communication generated by the surroundings and environment.

We will briefly describe the types of augmented communication systems that some children will use. It is essential for you to know what types of augmented communication systems the child is using to ensure there is a continuity of approach.

31

There are many variations on the market and some children find it difficult to determine what the sign or symbol means when it is not the same as the one they use, perhaps at school or at home.

Let's start at the beginning. What is non-verbal communication?

It may seem an easy question but perhaps there is more to this than meets the eye? (metaphorical language!)

> **After Catherine was caught shoplifting, her parents needed her to understand how important it was that she should not do it again. To ensure she understood, her parents requested a police officer to come to the house in full uniform to explain what would happen if she did this again and to give her a chance to explain to him about the bullies. Catherine would not have recognised a police officer if he was in plain clothes; she needed the additional non-verbal communication of a uniform.**

Non-verbal communication can be intentional or unintentional; it can broadly be broken down into two areas and into the five senses.
Firstly, **messages given by the sender** include:

- Touch
- Proximity
- Gestures and body movement
- Posture
- Signing
- Facial expressions
- A glance or eye contact, including gazing
- Noise and the volume of noise
- Vocal noises (known as paralanguage) such as cough, shout, scream, moan, whine, yawn, laugh, cry, belch
- Silence or pauses in speech
- Intonation of voice
- Syntax (choice of words used)
- Dress
- Smell
- Taste

32

Secondly, **messages given by or introduced to the environment,** again either intentional or unintentional.

- The use of symbols or photographs
- The written word or pictorial representation
- Posters, rules, signs
- Objects of reference
- Situational experience
  (what is happening at the time)

These are not exhaustive lists. Non-verbal communication is around us all the time, making up more than 90% of our understanding of the world.

Touch and proximity

It is important to recognise how our behaviour impacts on the way the child understands our intentions and therefore responds. What are the messages we want to achieve with touch? Why are we touching someone, and what meaning do we read when someone else touches us?

It is a very personal form of communication and may not be appropriate for all children on the spectrum. Some children may have an aversion to touch and may react unexpectedly. Check with the child's parents to see how they respond and react to touch.

Of course, we use touch in play all the time: during rough and tumble play, supporting a child to create a model, helping a child to climb or swing.

Be aware that some children will prefer a gentle touch and others a firm touch.

Some children will not wish you to invade their personal space or may not understand your own or other children's personal space.

When Catherine was young, she enjoyed regular cuddles with her parents and friends.

She did not understand the concept of personal space and was unable to read unspoken messages when people did not want her near them.

She gets on better with adults and tends to focus all her attention on one individual rather than play with everyone. This behaviour can become obsessive; ignoring others in favour of just one person.

At her local after school club Catherine has built a good relationship with a male play worker, James. James is happy to play with Catherine but is aware that at 13 it is not appropriate that she constantly wants to climb all over him, hold his hand and touch him.

James shares his concerns with his manager and together they have a quiet word with Mum, explaining the situation and agreeing a way forward by putting some clear boundaries in place.

Catherine is not happy about these boundaries but with support is able to understand the appropriate social unspoken rules of engagement.

It is important to set clear boundaries and rules around acceptable behaviour. Touch is a behaviour in itself. It may be okay to hug Mum, but not the play worker. Ensure the child understands that they are still special to you by using other ways of showing interest in them as an individual.

Some children may have an adversity to touching things that provide a sensory experience, or hate the feeling of something unusual such as finger paints, clay, mud, water or wet sand. During play, we try to encourage the use of non-representational materials to encourage imaginative play.

Christopher had an irrational fear of water. For some reason, he decided that water was scary. This meant that bath and wash times were a nightmare. For several months his parents battled with arguments, and his behaviour became almost uncontrollable. Christopher would drink through a straw, using a cup with a lid.

His parents decided that they needed to encourage him to play with water and began by using bubbles. Christopher was delighted to see bubbles floating in the air. He was encouraged to burst them with his hands.

Once he was used to bubbles and enjoyed bursting them, his parents introduced him to the concept of blowing bubbles using his straw. He understood this quickly, creating little bubbles for himself.

Next came blowing bigger bubbles in a bowl, using the straw as illustrated by his parents. When Christopher could see the water he would not go near it but, once the water was hidden beneath a film of bubbles, he was happy to participate. His parents encouraged him to burst the bubbles with one finger and he decided on his own to slap the bubbles with the palm of his hand.

Of course, his hand sank beneath the bubbles and he touched the water. His parents stood back, not knowing what to expect. However, Christopher could still not see the water and, unexpectedly, happily sloshed the bubbles backwards and forwards.

He is now happy to take a bubble bath, provided that no water is showing when he gets in. He has a range of bath toys that make a wide variety of bubbles, and his favourite activity is making giant bubbles in the garden.

Be aware of cultural differences. Many Asian cultures will not allow touching others. Muslims and Hindus generally will not touch with the left hand. In some cultures touching can only happen between the same genders. In some Asian cultures it is rude to touch the head as the head houses the soul. In other cultures people will not touch certain parts of their body. Be aware of the children you are working with and get to know them individually. If in doubt, ask!

Gestures, body language and postures

All children and young people on the spectrum will have a different level of understanding gestures and body language. Some children will be able to understand what is meant easily and to others gestures have no meaning at all. We know someone is interested in what we are saying if they lean towards us. For a child on the spectrum this may seem like a threat.

Emotions are particularly difficult for some children to read. What would your emotions look like if you just wanted to be left alone for a while? There may not be an obvious gesture or body language to illustrate this. However, if you are really happy and smile, the message becomes more apparent as your features change to reflect how you feel. Some children will need you to exaggerate gestures.

During play, we encourage children through the use of our voice and body language. Some children will respond to simple praise, and others will need further encouragement with exaggerated movements and tone of voice. Remember that body language includes physical touch such as kicking, punching or spitting, and this is how some children will give messages when they have no other means to do so.

Again, consider a cultural difference. For example, pointing with an index finger is considered rude by some Asian cultures, and, in Germany, pointing is normally undertaken by using the little finger.

> **When Mary was young she learned at her play school to show that she was happy by putting a thumb up or that she was sad by having a thumb down. This has continued into adulthood and is used constantly.**

his is a learnt behaviour used to express her feelings. For instance, if she feels someone is doing something wrong, she will express her feelings by automatically showing them a thumbs-down sign. She also uses these signs to ask others how they feel, especially if she cannot read the unspoken facial expressions. Within her residential home she'll ask others how they feel by putting her thumb up or down and wait for a response. When she was growing up, when she misbehaved, her parents would use the sign to ask her if she felt her behaviour was acceptable and repeat "good thing" or "bad thing". She would consider carefully and choose a response accordingly. Such a simple sign has allowed Mary to have a level of choice and control in her life.

Eye contact It is a mistake to think that all children on the autism spectrum have little or no eye contact. Indeed, some find eye contact very difficult and avoid looking at you, whereas others will look you in the eye with a prolonged gaze.

It is easy to think that a child is not focusing on what you are saying if they are not looking at you. This is our own assumption and is not necessarily accurate. If you are talking directly to another adult and they do not have eye contact with you there may be an assumption that they are being evasive or dishonest. In the Western world our culture requires us to 'speak with our eyes'.

For children who have difficulty reading emotion the eyes can be very frightening; messages may not be read easily and, to avoid misinterpretation or confusion, some children and young people will tend to avoid eye contact.

On the other hand (metaphorical language), some people on the autism spectrum will not let go of eye contact and this becomes uncomfortable for the other party. This is similar to a lack of understanding personal space.

 **When Catherine first started attending the play scheme she was frightened of eye contact and would not look any play worker in the face.**

She did not understand the messages they were giving. Instead, each day she brought with her a Sooty hand puppet and would talk through this without looking at the person she was talking to.

Her favourite phrase when asked to do something was: "Sooty says, 'I don't think so!'"

With encouragement, and once she had got to know the workers, Catherine began to interact and enjoy herself. Once she had built a relationship, the puppet stopped coming to the play scheme.

Noise

Many children on the autism spectrum dislike noise and will hide their head in their hands, put their fingers in their ears, or scream to make a sound that is louder than the ones they want to shut out.

Occasionally, you will find that children will shout at you to "stop talking!" Be aware of the sensitivities around sound. Be aware of how your own voice may sound to a child (remember the train travelling along the tracks).

Consider the other noises that are audible. The tick of a clock may be fascinating to the child and they will listen to that and cut out the sound of your voice. Some children will have noise sensitivities; certain pitches can be painful and will evoke reactions.

Many children enjoy noise as a calming method, particularly in the form of music. Singing favourite theme tunes can help reduce anxiety and help calm children down. It is all about knowing the individual children in your care, understanding their individuality and personal responses to noise.

Suminda loves music; she dances to any beat and will copy movements. Suminda finds waiting very difficult.

During a visit to a local animal farm she decided that she had had enough of waiting to feed the animals and wanted to go home.

She ran over to her play worker, Kate, looked at the visual symbols Kate had attached to her belt and found the symbol for home.

It was not possible to take Suminda back as she had come on a coach with other children. Suminda became very agitated. An ice cream did not help and her behaviour became dangerous to other children.

Her play worker began to sing "Head, shoulders, knees and toes" quietly, doing the actions. Within five minutes, Suminda was quiet and joining in. She happily spent the rest of the day at the farm.

Have you ever smelt the sea, or had a bad experience and smelt a landfill site or very smelly shoes? Smells can be very powerful or subtle.

Some children will use smells to make sense of the world and will sniff people to see if they like them. This can be very disconcerting, even if you are aware that this is a particular trait that the child uses.

Christopher is unable to tell you that he needs the toilet. It is not just that he is non-verbal, but that he cannot physically feel the sensation of having a full bladder or bowel. However, he is very sensitive to smells and when his pad is changed will always try to smell it.

His play worker has used his interest in smells and expanded his play opportunities by using smell as a play experience. To encourage Christopher to play with touch, sounds and sight, she created a range of 'smelly socks', containing items that smelt strongly such as coffee, sweets and fruit. She also added in things that made sounds such as scrunchy paper, pasta and bells.

While smelling the socks, Christopher was also encouraged to feel, see and hear the items.

Christopher also has 'learnt behaviour'. On occasion, rather than taking him to the toilet, staff check to see if he needs changing by having a 'quick sniff'. Christopher now thinks this is acceptable and will sniff both adults' and children's bottoms. Be aware of your own behaviour; what are you teaching the child?

 Many children on the autism spectrum have distinct likes and dislikes in relation to taste. Some children will only eat certain foods, liking or disliking taste, texture, or colour. Again, be aware of the individual, but keep trying new foods. Some children will enjoy creating food models that can be eaten afterwards, and trying new tastes that are not laid out in the form of a meal on a plate. Have a go at playing with food.

The environment

The environment gives out messages in many ways. Consider your setting: is it inviting and friendly, or is it confusing and far too stimulating for a child on the spectrum? We must remember that play is for all, not just for the child who happens to have an impairment. Although it is essential that we make adaptations to include all children, they must not be detrimental to other children's enjoyment and ability to play. All children have a right to play.

It is important to recognise what aspects of the environment provide non-verbal communication. For parents of disabled children it may be very hard to leave their child in the care of others, as indicated in the 'barriers to play' identified by parents. The venue needs to feel welcoming by having inclusive posters, public view of the Safeguarding Policy and examples of certificates for inclusion training displayed. This will support the parent to feel confident and know they are leaving their child in a suitable environment with trained staff.

Some parents will be looking particularly for safety, especially if their child does not recognise danger; some will be looking for evidence of understanding augmented communication systems with examples of pictures, signs and symbols.

If a child on the autism spectrum is about to start at your setting, consider displaying something they will be familiar with. Perhaps pictures or a poster of something that you know is of special interest. Have you got clear, positive rules on display, written by the children themselves, and preferably with an additional visual indicator to support understanding?

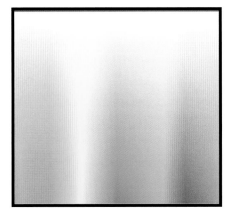

Consider quiet areas: are they bright, exciting and vibrant? Is it the same area that you use for time out?

This can be confusing to a child on the spectrum. Quiet, calming areas need to be low-arousal areas, where stimulation of senses is reduced.

We have already heard about an aversion to the colour red. Pale blues, lilacs, pale greens, creams, pale yellow and white are calming colours.

Some children may learn that, if they behave in a certain way, they will be taken to the 'time out area'. Actually, this is what the child wants to happen and the behaviour is undertaken specifically to achieve this result. Be aware of the communication behind the behaviour.

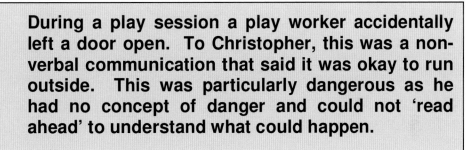

During a play session a play worker accidentally left a door open. To Christopher, this was a non-verbal communication that said it was okay to run outside. This was particularly dangerous as he had no concept of danger and could not 'read ahead' to understand what could happen.

Christopher uses a variety of non-verbal communication to get his message across, and will 'read' non-verbal communication to make sense of the world.

Remember the story of Christopher using his play worker as a tool to open the play dough.

Types of symbols, signs and systems

The most important consideration here is continuity of approach.

Before introducing a communication system find out if the child is already using some form of non-verbal communication, where, what and how it is being used. You do not necessarily need to be an 'expert', but ensure you are using the system in the correct manner. Explore websites, and research the names of systems to find out further information.

Sign language is very similar to other language in that it has dialects and accents which may vary regionally. Be aware of what the child is using and understands. The symbols below come from Communicate in Print available from www.widgit.com

Wait   Biscuit   Drink

Examples of the most commonly used augmented communication systems

PECS

PECS stands for Picture Exchange Communication System. In its simplest form the method is designed to support understanding by providing a visual illustration of an object. A child or young person picks up a picture of something, and hands it to an adult in exchange for what is on the card. A simple example may be of a picture of a cup being exchanged for a drink.

Each time a visual image is used the adult uses verbal sentences or words. The aim is to reduce the reliance upon the visual image and replace it by using verbal communication.

There are various stages to PECS, supporting children to develop simple sentences and more complex communication.

Makaton

There are a number of different sign languages used across the UK; Makaton is a very well-known communication system that encompasses signs and symbols. All Makaton symbols and signs are to be used alongside verbal communication.

The system is not there to replace words, but encourages children to participate in the use of words alongside the signs and symbols. It offers a structured approach to support communication. The signing used within Makaton is similar to BSL. Every drawn symbol has a corresponding sign that replicates the meaning.

"Hello" or "Goodbye"

British Sign Language (BSL)

BSL has been around for a considerable time. The first evidence appears in 1576 where a wedding was conducted in sign. It was recognised as a language in its own right in 1974. It is unlikely that children will use a true form of BSL unless they have a recognised hearing impairment or they are signing to support other friends or family members who are deaf. There are a great deal of similarities between BSL and other signing systems.

Signalong

Signalong is based on British Sign Language and is a system developed specifically for children and young people in 1992. It is not intended to replace speech; it is a total communications system and looks at the 'whole message' being passed from one person to another.

Teacch

Teacch (Treatment and Education of Autistic and related Communication handicapped Children) provides research and training in relation to autism based in North Carolina. Part of the training and guidance offered looks at the use of non-verbal communication to support children on the autism spectrum. For further information see www.autism.org.uk/teacch

Some schools use the Teacch approach; methodologies used within this approach can be suitable for a range of environments including play and free-time activities. The programmes use a wide range of ideas to support children's understanding including symbol cards and photographs of objects. There are many more systems in use. Be aware of what the individual child is using.

Note: Some children will not recognise drawn symbols as a representation of an object and will prefer to work with photographs that accurately reflect the specific object or activity. Photographs are useful to use in visual timetables.

Suminda wants to know when her mum is coming to pick her up from a play scheme. She gets upset and stressed if she does not know what is going to happen next and, if the play workers do not prepare her, she will express her feelings in a display of challenging behaviour.

The play workers use symbol cards to let Suminda know what is going to happen during the day, creating a schedule of activities. Towards the end of the day they need to ensure Suminda has been to the toilet, has her shoes on and is ready to be collected by Mum.

If this does not happen and Suminda is interrupted in her play she can become very violent and refuse to leave what she is doing.

 Mum has provided the staff with a number of appropriate symbol cards that Suminda recognises and uses at home.

However, the symbol for 'car' is represented by a line drawing. Suminda does not recognise this as 'Mum's car' and requires the use of a photograph to represent her own car, not just any car.

There are many different types of symbol cards on the market today. It is possible to purchase computer programmes to print your own symbols such as Widget and Rebus or to purchase pre-made symbol cards.

It is worth enquiring in your own area to see if any schools or voluntary organisations have an online system that will allow you to choose the words you wish to have symbolised. This may be a service available free of charge or at low cost. It is especially important to use the same symbols that are already used with the child or young person to ensure continuity of approach.

Depending on the individual requirements of the child, it may be possible to draw your own images or use Clip Art, instead of purchasing expensive systems.

Some children have difficulty in ordering and sequencing, dislike change, and require structure and routine. Symbol cards can be used to create schedules or timetables. This non-verbal form of communication helps their understanding of what is going to happen next, and can support the child to understand what choices they may have.

This is particularly useful in the play environment where a child may get distraught when faced with too much choice. By providing the child with two or three choices, indicated by symbol cards and backed up verbally, it encourages the child to make a decision about what they wish to do.

play music

or

build with bricks

The symbols will generally be attached by a small hook and loop tab to a board. This allows the child to choose which activity he would like to do, and the other alternative is taken off the board for later. Symbols can also be used for instruction such as the one below.

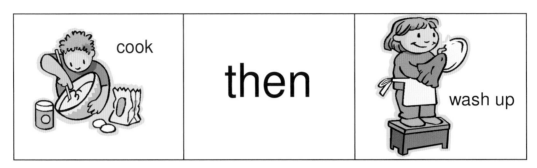

Objects of Reference

Objects of reference are also known as signifiers. As previously discussed, they work very well to support understanding. Firstly, identify the activity that can be supported by the use of a signifier. It can be as diverse as holding up a nappy or pad to signify time to go to the toilet, or holding up a crayon to signify drawing.

In the same way as the symbols, objects of reference can provide a mechanism for the individual to make a choice about what play activities they wish to take part in. Some children will learn and replicate by bringing you an object, signifying that they want to do an activity.

It is worth considering the object itself. Is it unique to a particular activity or could it be used in a number of activities? Does the child recognise it as symbolic of the activity, or is it your choice? Can the child or young person pick it up and hold it and take it to the activity?

Within the play environment there needs to be an introduction of the object to associate it with the play opportunity.

Draw attention to the object of reference. Allow the child to hold it in their hands and use language to support the link between the object and the play activity.

For instance, give the child a building brick and say: "Let's go and build..."

Once the activity has finished, it is important that the object is put away so that it does not confuse the child. Do not leave the bricks out; put them away. Some children may use a 'finished box', a cardboard or plastic box where non-verbal forms of communication are put once the task has been completed.

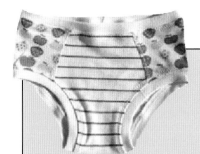

Suminda uses symbols and signs to help support her understanding.

Each morning she has a schedule to follow that enables her to get dressed on her own.

A picture of each item of clothing is printed on to a small card, which is attached by Velcro to a board on the wall. When she has put on an item of clothing, she takes the card off the board and puts it in a 'finished' box.

One day, her mum realised that she had spent a long time getting dressed and was not yet down for breakfast. On going upstairs she realised that Suminda had forgotten to take the visual symbol off the wall and put it in her finished box.

Every time she had gone back to the wall having put on the piece of clothing illustrated, she went back and put on an identical piece of clothing again.

When her mum walked into the bedroom Suminda was wearing six pairs of knickers!

Children may need support to understand how to use these systems. They are very useful in play settings, and can be utilised for all children, not just those on the autism spectrum.

It is worth reiterating the importance of continuity. If the child is already using an augmented communication system, use the same symbols. Ask the school or parents where the symbols are available from.

So why is non-verbal communication so important?

Non-verbal communication is used to enable the child or young person to understand and make sense of the world around them.

It can be used to repeat or reinforce the verbal message, and support children's understanding. It allows children to: make choices; increase options; make decisions for themselves; and communicate their requirements to you.

Non-verbal communication can also be a good way of ensuring that the child or young person enjoyed the activities on offer.

Children who have little verbal communication should be given an opportunity to express their feelings. A useful way of doing this is to provide an activity evaluation sheet using visual symbols. Encourage the child to place an appropriate emotion face against the activity, indicating how much they enjoyed it.

	It was great	It was OK	I did not like it

This activity can also help children to relate emotions against facial expressions. Some children will need to see photographs of real people showing facial expressions rather than caricatures.

These sheets can provide a snapshot into the world of the child. If the child is unable to tell you if they want to do an activity you are suggesting, have a look back and see what the child enjoys doing.

There are many useful resources available to provide support. Consider using a digital camera to take pictures of children participating in activities that they enjoy, and create a scrapbook. Use the book to offer choice and control to children and young people by identifying what they would like to do. Photos can also be used to support children's understanding of what is going to happen next.

Consider the cone inside a cotton reel. What could this non-representational item be used for in relation to play?

Perhaps you thought of:
- A telescope
- A megaphone
- A wand
- A bat to hit a ball
- A marker for a game of football
- The beak of a duck
- The body of a puppet

Play is only limited by our own imagination. Loose parts play uses non-representational items that have no immediate play value to encourage imaginative activities. Children on the autism spectrum may find it difficult to imagine what something could be used for beyond its known use.

The third triad of impairment looks at the lack of imagination and how some children may present this trait.

This trait can result in literal thinking and difficulty thinking 'outside the box' (metaphorical language). Some children and young people get frightened when they do not know what is going to happen next. This fear can be exhibited through challenging behaviour, particularly if they have few other means of communication.

This lack of imagination impacts on all areas of play and cannot be isolated from the traits of social interaction and social communication.

Some of the short case studies and stories have already made reference to this trait. Think back through the stories. What have you recognised already? Good communication reduces the fear of the unknown.

This section focuses on how the lack of imagination impacts on children's play, and provides ideas to support creative play using the children's own special interests.

A literal understanding

 **Christopher enjoys activities that are repetitive and produce the same effect each time they are undertaken. He does not like surprises, particularly loud noises such as balloons being burst.**

One of his favourite activities is to turn a toy car upside down and spend hours spinning the car's wheels while humming. He is very happy undertaking this activity and if the car is taken away he will show his displeasure by spitting and hitting.

His parents are very concerned that he will not gain many benefits from this activity and want to encourage him to reduce his reliance upon the car and start to experiment with different types of play.

Christopher's play worker, Roshni, was given the challenge to think about exploring new avenues for play.

Initially, Roshni spent some time observing Christopher's play to identify exactly what he was doing. She realised that it was not the car that attracts Christopher but the movement of the spinning wheels. He does not relate the object in his hand to a car that travels on a road. He does not have the imagination to race it around a track or squeal to a halt to fill up with fuel.

She began to put together some thoughts about things that spin, and came up with:

- Waterwheels
- Windmills
- Tyres
- Hoops
- Spinning tops
- Yo-yos
- Helicopter blades

- Merry-go- rounds
- Roller skates
- Fans
- Food mixers
- Clothes in a washing machine
- Maple seeds

This gave her a start to consider some new ideas.

Roshni decided to experiment with a range of new ideas, introducing them one by one to Christopher. Initially, she used a small hoop, playing with it in front of Christopher so that he could get used to it.

She rolled it along the floor and spun it around like spinning a coin. She also put it around her waist to use as a hula hoop.

Once Christopher had expressed an interest in what she was doing, she took the hoop outside on to the grass and rolled it away from her, asking Christopher to roll it back. After a while, Christopher got the hang of it and spent a happy half hour rolling the hoop backwards and forwards. This was a big step, as Christopher did not normally 'play' or 'interact' with other children or adults.

Next, Roshni tied some ribbons to the hoop so that when it rolled the ribbons flew out in the breeze. Christopher was fascinated with the ribbons and enjoyed the sensation of them running over his hand while the hoop was rolling.

Roshni now tied small bells to the ribbons so that as the hoop rolled it made a sound. Initially, Christopher did not like this; it was not the same, but with patience Roshni encouraged him to roll the hoop himself and introduced a short stick to run along with and keep the hoop rolling. As she ran along, Christopher watched and followed her with his eyes. This was a good breakthrough as it showed a direct interest. Roshni gave him the stick and showed him how to run and keep the hoop rolling. Christopher began to run, watching the hoop and ribbons and listening to the bells.

The benefits of this play using the initial obsession of watching a spinning wheel include:

- Social: beginning to respond to Roshni and engaging with play
- Physical: playing outside and running
- Communication: although limited, the activity enabled Christopher to express his emotions and enjoyment through participation, particularly through laughter.
- The introduction of sensory play through the feel of the ribbons and sound of the bells

Using the other ideas that Roshni had, what other play activities could be explored? Consider previous case studies and Christopher's enjoyment of playing with bubbles. Can this be incorporated into his enjoyment of things that spin?

Suminda's parents wanted her to enjoy her birthday and decided to organise a party. They were determined that she would have the same kind of party as other children.

They blew up balloons, decorated the house and organised games. They invited friends and family to attend and also booked a bouncy castle and a clown.

On the day of the party everything seemed to be going well: the day was fine; guests arrived. However, Suminda was nowhere to be seen.

There was lots of loud noise, bright lights, brightly coloured balloons and people that Suminda did not know. No one had explained to her what was going to happen; she was frightened of the attention and scared of the bouncy castle and the clown.

Suminda was eventually found hiding beneath the dining room table, cowering in a corner.

Suminda's parents had only wanted to do the best they could for their daughter. They wanted her to have the same kind of experiences as other children.

When planning activities it is important to recognise our own expectations of how a child will respond. Are they based on an assumption of a child's likes and dislikes, or do we consider the child's individual personality and how they respond to certain stimuli?

It is good to provide new play experiences for children. Some children on the spectrum will need some preparation so that they are not afraid of something they do not know.

Whose needs, wishes and wants was this activity planned for? Suminda's parents wanted to give her something that other children would enjoy. They had planned the day for Suminda. However, they had not taken account of how the traits of autism present for her. Suminda has a fear of too many people, has sensitivities and does not like too many bright colours and noise.

Her fear transferred into behaviour, and she hid from what she was frightened of. Her behaviour was a form of communication, saying: "Go away; you are scaring me."

Be aware of your own expectations when working with children on the autism spectrum. Prepare for the unexpected, and prepare the children for the activities by introducing things slowly, using appropriate communication strategies. Suminda enjoys music and being with her immediate family. She also enjoys going on a bouncy castle. The party, however, was all too much for her. Perhaps her birthday could still have involved the activities but on a smaller scale where she was not subjected to sensory overload.

> **Mary takes language very literally and will undertake any instructions given. On being asked to take the clothes on the airer upstairs, she did so, literally carrying the entire airer full of clothes upstairs, where she put it on the bed. The instructions were not clear enough.**

We need to consider our own language. How could the request be rephrased to allow Mary to understand? What about: "Mary, please take the clothes off the airer, fold them up and take them upstairs and put them on my bed"? (Note: 'my bed' provides clarity of which bed to put the clothes on).

The next story involves Catherine. Catherine enjoys life and tries her hardest to fit in. Sometimes, she finds it difficult to understand what to do in social situations and she will copy others' speech and behaviour to try and 'get it right'. She sees the world in black and white. Things are right or they are wrong. She cannot see that how other people behave is not necessarily acceptable; therefore, she is happy to copy.

53

Catherine wanted a disco for her birthday party. The village hall was duly booked, the disco set up and friends invited.

She was thrilled, got herself dressed and arrived at the hall. When she arrived, she sat down at the side of the hall and watched others arrive and begin to dance.

She did not have the social skills to invite herself to dance at her own disco. She needed encouragement to get up and enter the social fray.

Scott, a friend from school, asked her to dance. Catherine was pleased. Her body language expressed her delight in being asked to dance. However, she was still very uncertain at how to behave and looked around at the others to ensure she was doing the right thing. This meant that no attention was being paid to Scott. He was ignored as Catherine copied others' behaviour and actions.

Catherine's mother was standing in the kitchen looking through the hatch. In the corner, she spied a couple getting very amorous and, as the girl's hand slid towards the boy's bottom, she thought to herself: 'No Catherine, don't look over there'.

Unfortunately, Catherine looked at exactly that same scene. She then thought that the behaviour she saw was what she needed to do. Scott was somewhat surprised that Catherine, who had been paying him no attention, suddenly planted her hands very firmly on his buttocks!

After the dance, Scott did not ask her to dance again and Catherine did not understand why. She had done exactly what she had seen others doing.

Catherine's mum had to have a quiet word after the disco, explaining appropriate behaviour. Catherine learned her lesson, but only in the context of a disco in the village hall. It was very difficult for her to transpose that learning into another situation.

We have previously mentioned metaphorical language. Be aware of the children you are working with, get to know them and understand how best to use language.

Taking things literally can relate to all aspects of life. Some children on the spectrum will find it very hard when things do not happen at the time expected; they may get upset if someone is off sick and is not working when the child expects it. Not knowing what will happen next can be very disturbing.

Ferai, a young man living in a residential home, loved walking. However, when Theresa, his personal assistant, suggested going for a walk, Ferai clung to the doorframe, obviously very frightened. Theresa did not know what the matter was and shared the experience with her manager.

Her manager offered the following comments: "Does Ferai know where he is going, how long he will be out or if he is going to get back in time for tea? Taking it further, does he know he will actually be coming back or if he will see his mum again?"

Theresa considered this and tried a new approach: "Ferai," she said, "would you like to come for a walk to the end of the lane and back again?" Ferai gladly held her hand and skipped out of the door looking forward to his walk.

Here, Ferai was scared of the unknown. A very simple statement explaining what will happen reduced the fear and enabled him to participate in an activity he enjoys. Put this into the context of a school play time: "We will go outside to play. When the whistle is blown we will be coming back inside."

Suminda lives at the top of a hill. Each day, when she knew it was time to leave for school, she misbehaved, doing anything to stop having to leave the house.

In exasperation, her mum eventually asked her why she did not want to leave the house. "I don't want to see the little people," she said. "What little people?" her mum responded, confused.

"The little people that live in the little houses at the bottom of the hill."

Suminda had taken the perspective of houses on a hill very literally. She could not appreciate that, as things were further away, they looked smaller, and the nearer they were, the bigger they looked. In her mind's eye, if the houses were small, then the people that lived in them must also be very small. She was scared of the unknown.

All it took eventually was to ask the question. Suminda's mum was then able to recognise that the fear was real and that there was a reason. Reassurance was needed. A walk down the hill to see the small houses getting bigger and Suminda was then happy to leave the house. Remember, sometimes it only takes a question to find out what is concerning children!

Reading emotions

It can be very difficult for people on the autism spectrum to read emotions and understand how they themselves are feeling. Remember the illustration of Sam falling off the swing? Catherine had no empathy for her injury. It is important to explain to children on the spectrum how their actions can hurt others' feelings.

When Joseph was younger, he learnt to say sorry if he had hit someone because he knew it hurt. He did not know that he could hurt people's feelings by what was said as there were no physical marks.

Joseph was very truthful and would say what he saw. This often caused embarrassment such as a loud question to a pregnant lady in a supermarket: "Why are you so fat?"

His parents worked alongside his educational physiologist to develop a system whereby, if he hurt someone's feelings at home, they would hold their hand over their heart in pretend pain and say: "Gosh, you really hurt my feelings." This way, Joseph learned that words can hurt and he began to ask his mum if it was okay for him to say something. Although Joseph does not always get it right, he tries hard to fit in, in a social context. It is not always easy and, on occasion, he gets frustrated and finds it hard to understand others.

Mary has difficulty in withdrawing from others' feelings and emotions. If someone is angry, she gets very angry on their behalf and cannot see the situation from an independent viewpoint. If someone she is close to is happy, then you can guarantee she will be happy too. However, if someone near to her is hiding their feelings and is actually really upset, she will not be able to read their feelings and act appropriately. She will instead respond to that individual in the way she did when she was last with them, taking their last known emotion as a standard unless someone tells her differently or the emotion portrayed is clearly visible for her to recognise.

Consider this in a play environment. Children may need to be supported to understand emotions. Try a game of Simon Says. Instead of saying: "Simon says touch your toes", play a game of "Simon says be happy", "Simon says be sad" and other emotions. Exaggerate the facial expressions that would be used to express the desired emotion.

Some children may use emotion cards to help them express their feelings; others may find it easier to use puppets to explore emotions through a third party, or use echolalic phrases such as 'Mrs Goggins is very cross today' (from the *Postman Pat* series of stories).

Social stories are a useful way to explore how others may be feeling or to explore appropriate behaviour. Social stories can be made simply by using Clip Art. The story below was written for Suminda to explain what else she could do when she feels angry, rather than kick other people.

Getting Angry

Angry

no   hitting

scribble

Happy

Everyone gets angry sometimes.
When Mum gets angry she might shout,
When Mrs Chikore gets angry she may say: "STOP!"
When Jackie gets angry she scribbles in red crayon,
When Ben gets angry he tears up bits of paper.
They do not hit other people when they are angry;
They use words or acceptable actions to say how they feel.
If I get angry, I could say: "I feel angry". This will make me feel better. If I get angry, I could draw a picture about what I am angry about. If I get angry, I could tear up paper.

Mum or Mrs Chikore will try to help me.
It's okay to feel angry. It is not okay to hit or bite other people. It is better to be happy and smile.

> Mary takes life very literally and shows little emotion. When someone dies in the care home where she works she does not get upset.
>
> One day she phoned home and, on being asked if she had had a good day, said: "No, not really." When asked what had happened, she told her mother that one of her residents had died while she had been feeding her at lunchtime.
>
> Mary's mother automatically responded: "Gosh, what did you do?"
>
> Mary's response was: "I said: 'Oh, bye then!'"

This may make you smile, but the story illustrates again how some people on the spectrum see things in black and white. For Mary, someone is alive or dead. She does not get upset or particularly emotional unless she is exhibiting echolalic behaviour and is upset because someone else is.

Children on the autism spectrum have diverse responses to death. Some may be fascinated about how a body decomposes; others may ask for permission to be sad, which lasts for a few minutes before they are fine again. They have been sad. Why should they continue being sad, and why are others still sad?

During play, emotions may be replayed so that the child can make sense of them. Playing at dying, being dead, or playing funerals should not be stopped. Through play the child can come to terms with a loss and make sense of the world, even if the play is not what you might expect.

> Nadeem attended her grandfather's funeral. While waiting for the car to arrive, Nadeem recognised that there was a lot of emotion in the room.
>
> No one was crying and there were no visual indicators to give her a clue to help her identify how she should respond or feel. It was as though she carried a bag of emotions, and she dipped her hand in, pulling one out to join in.
>
> Unfortunately, she pulled out laughter and began to laugh, which was not appropriate. Her dad took her out, but as people began to cry she was able to copy and join in.

Other potential features

Over the past few chapters we have explored in detail the triad of impairment. There are other possible ways in which autism will present. Children may display a range of behaviours that are stereotypical of autism, including:

Physical

- Body movements such as head banging, spinning, flapping, circling, rocking, putting hands over ears and tapping, among others
- Some children may have 'stiff fingers', holding their fingers out straight, rather than bending them. Some children may not swing their arms and legs properly when walking, resulting in a 'stiff gait' or usual walk/run; or may walk on tiptoe
- Some children may run away, or climb beyond the boundaries of safety
- Children may have difficulty in physical games. This may be because they are uncoordinated, clumsy and have poor gross and/or fine motor skills. Dyspraxia is often associated with autism

Repetitive behaviours

- Listening to particular noises such as a washing machine, a kettle boiling or a clock ticking
- Switching lights or other appliances on and off
- Placing objects in a long line; the child will get upset if the objects are moved
- Placing books and DVDs in order, based on colour, size, title or author or something else entirely
- Complex bedtime and other routines. The routine needs to remain the same for the child. Changes in routine can cause severe upset and frustration
- Mealtime routines and eating habits. Some children will only eat certain foods, colours, textures and brands. They may wish to always sit at the same place and have the same items on the table

Attachments

- Many children will build an attachment to an unusual object such as a tin of polish or a shoe brush; the list is endless. Other children will go from object to object but, whichever is the current attachment, it cannot be replaced by another object that is similar. Some children will collect strange objects and hoard them; examples include empty toilet roll tubes, grass cuttings, or their own hair from haircuts
- Children (and adults) on the higher functioning end of the spectrum (Aspergers Syndrome) may have a fascination with numbers, stars, the weather and certain animals (dinosaurs are a favourite)

Responses to sensory stimuli

This has partially been explored in previous chapters. Further examples include:

- Reaction to loud noise
- Constant repetition of favourite theme tune or other favourite sound
- Response to bright lights, bright colours and certain types of lighting
- Response to certain smells. Some children may need to stop and smell new objects or people as they pass
- Low or high pain thresholds

When Joseph was 4 years old, his mum scalded herself badly and her hand came up in very nasty blisters. She showed Joseph her hand, saying: "Ouch, hurt, hot," indicating the kettle to let Joseph know that he must never touch the kettle.

Instead of paying attention to the kettle, he was fascinated with the blisters on her hand.

Later in the day, Joe's mum walked into the kitchen to find him pouring boiling water over his own hand. Joe wanted to have the same blisters. He felt no pain at all but was upset that his mum took him to the hospital and the blisters were covered up!

Behavioural traits

- Screaming in public places, especially where the child is frightened, confused or upset, leading to fear and anxiety
- Physical response to change, including clinging on to furniture, objects or people
- Stating the obvious and being too truthful can upset others, for instance: "You smell!"
- Destructive and aggressive behaviour, for example, destroying others' work if it is the wrong colour or the child just does not like it for some unknown reason

Some of these behaviours may last into adulthood. They may change depending on the development of the individual.

Savant autism

Less than 2% of people diagnosed with autism may have a special talent or gift known as savant autism. However, many members of the public focus on these talents due to media representation of autism.

Talents will vary. Examples include:

- Ability to draw
- Memory for numbers
- Ability to play a musical instrument
- Ability to copy voices (including singing voices)
- Computer programming

The list is not exhaustive. It is said that many geniuses were on the autism spectrum, including Einstein.

Chapter Four:
A bit about play

'Play' is a word we use all the time. As mentioned in Chapter One, we expect children to respond, react and play naturally. This is not always so for the child on the autism spectrum. There are various definitions of play that have been used over the years. A clear, short version reads:

> **What children & young people do when they follow their own ideas and interests in their own way and for their own reasons!**
> Getting Serious About Play (DCMS 2004)

It is important to hear the child or young person's voice, so this is what they said play is:

> **"Play is what I do when my mum is not looking!"** (8-year-old boy)
>
> **"Play is something that has to be exciting, adventurous, that gets your adrenaline pumping and heart racing."** (18-year-old girl)
>
> **"I use my free-time to hang out with my mates and going fishing."** (14-year-old boy)

Three children on the autism spectrum were also asked what they felt play was:

> **"Play is watching *Thomas the Tank Engine*!"** (8-year-old boy)
> **"Play is something I do on my computer."** (12-year-old girl)
> **"I read books about Astronomy."** (14-year-old boy)

We all still play in our own way. As adults we generally call it a hobby. If we analyse why we do what we do, we get the answer: "Because I enjoy it." We don't necessarily enjoy being forced to undertake a hobby or activity that is not our strength or one where we don't like participating. Should we therefore be forcing types of play on to children on the autism spectrum if they do not like what they are being asked to do?

62

Benefits of play

There are many benefits associated with play. What we learn through play as a child can be applied to adulthood, for example, where did you first learn:

- **Social skills**
- **Creative thinking and imagination**
- **Communication skills**
- Physical endurance, balance, judgement
- How to handle emotions
- Good people skills
- Ability to plan
- Ability to see others' point of view
- Resilience, ability to get up and start again when things go wrong
- Confidence
- Co-operation
- Planning activities
- Resolution of conflict

Take another look at the first three listed and consider the triad of impairment. Providing children on the autism spectrum with the opportunity to play freely is essential if we are to encourage development in these three areas.

Children on the spectrum may need extra support and encouragement: to play with others; to play imaginatively and creatively; and to understand the unspoken social rules of engagement.

Play also helps children on the autism spectrum to learn:

- Appropriate behaviour
- Task completion
- Turn taking
- Building relationships
- Appropriate language
- Tolerance to a variety of ways to play with toys
- Reciprocal interaction
- **But most of all to have fun!**

How does play differ for children on the autism spectrum?

Of course, children on the autism spectrum still need to play, but they may not give out the types of play signals that you expect from other children.

Children on the spectrum may:

- Lack spontaneous make-believe play or social imitative play
- Prefer sensory motor play beyond the verbal or mental age of the child (for example, still mouthing objects)
- Have little or no symbolic play (using objects for something other than their original use) and lack pretend play (make-believe)
- Prefer literal play
- Prefer to play on their own or may need encouragement to join in and be a part of group play
- Have echolalic play (a lack of imaginative play, instead copying others' play patterns, behaviours and words)
- Display ritualistic play (using objects and toys in a static manner without consideration for their play purpose, instead looking at the object rather than play potential, for example, spinning the wheels on a toy car rather than playing with the toy car itself)
- Prefer interest-based play – children on the autism spectrum often have specific interests such as dinosaurs, trains, the environment, space. These are only a few examples; play can be dominated by these obsessions.

Children on the spectrum may get frustrated when too much choice is given in the play offer. Instead they may prefer a structured or semi-structured play environment which provides limited choice in a way that is appropriate for the individual. This may be by providing two or three choices through picture symbols, signs, and schedule boards or by using objects of reference. Remember, it is important to take away the unchosen activity so that the child can concentrate on the play in hand.

Do not restrict the types of play available to children on the spectrum; they should have the same choice as others. Just consider how the play offer is made, making it appropriate to the individual.

Chapter Five:
The role of the adult in play

The role of the adult or play worker is to facilitate, encourage, support and enhance play for children. This is no different for children on the autism spectrum. The following chapter explores what this may mean to children on the autism spectrum.

Adults involved in children's play must consider how adaptations need to take place to allow the child to fully participate in the play setting or specific activity. Think back on what you have learnt so far through this book. The adaptations may need to be in the form of a physical change, social change or in the way we communicate. We may need to consider the environment or particular stimuli or sensory experience that a child is sensitive to.

We may need to adapt the activities and base them around the child's specific interest. It is important to introduce new activities and to encourage the child to take part where they are unsure.

Challenge:

Suminda is fascinated by *Thomas the Tank Engine*. Her world revolves around watching DVDs and lining up toy trains, and she enjoys singing the theme tune, which she finds very comforting.

How can you include this special interest to encourage:

- **Sensory play using sand?**
- **A social activity that involves sharing?**
- **A creative activity that encourages imagination?**

Our first sentence in this chapter said that the role of the adult is to enhance play for children. How could you enhance play, where play seems so limited?

It is important for adults to ensure the play process takes precedence. Many children on the spectrum will push others away, preferring to play on their own. It is easy to lead children into an adult-led agenda, particularly if they are not imaginative. Try to encourage children to think of ideas for themselves.

Adults should consider the environment, supporting children and young people to create a space in which they can play. Adults can encourage imaginative play through the introduction of loose parts such as material, junk and scrap. These are items have no intrinsic or immediate play value, but can be used in play.

When you were a child did you ever turn a chair upside down and pretend it was a rocket or submarine? Even though a child on the autism spectrum may only see the chair as a chair, we can encourage a broader use of imagination through the use of pictures and stories.

It is important to understand that children on the spectrum may not recognise other children's space, and their general spatial awareness may be poor.

All children enjoy secret places, dens, hideouts, corners and dark places. For some children on the spectrum these spaces are very important, allowing areas for time out, calming down or for reducing the sensory overload. Small pop-up tents are invaluable, transportable and light, and can be folded down easily. They can be used as mini low-arousal areas.

One child enjoyed climbing and hiding in trees. Up there, no one disturbed him and he was able to watch others without having to join in. All adults working with children on the autism spectrum should understand the child's individual requirements, particularly in relation to communication systems used. With good communication, preparation and planning the child's play experience can be greatly enhanced by the adult.

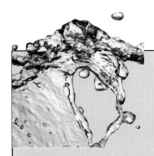

For the first time ever, Suminda was going swimming with her summer play scheme. Her play worker had shown her pictures of the pool and her swimming costume.

When they arrived, Suminda happily got changed and thoroughly enjoyed herself. She surprised everybody by splashing and screaming with enjoyment in the water.

When the time came to get out and go home, Suminda got into the shower but at that point held on tightly to the water pipes. She would not leave the shower.

Her play worker tried to support her understanding of what was happening next by talking to her, holding up her towel and clothes. This did not work so she tried bribery by holding up a biscuit. Next, she used a symbol card to represent the play setting. Suminda got more and more distressed.

The play leader was aware of the situation; she came and stood in front of the shower. "Suminda," she said, "time for the bus". At the same time the play leader used two very simple signs: time and bus. Suminda let go of the pipes, held the play leader's hand and happily went to get changed.

Here, the play worker had tried her hardest to communicate with Suminda. However, she was receiving sensory overload with the sound and smells of the pool and changing room. As she became distressed, her own ability to recognise the communication given was diminished. The play worker was also stressed as she tried her hardest to communicate. She began to overload Suminda with too many words and too many types of communication at the same time.

The play leader recognised that Suminda needed very simple, clear and easy to understand communication about what would happen next. Suminda knew that the bus would take her back to the play setting as she had come to the pool on the bus. She also knew that she could not get on the bus in her costume, so these additional steps and instructions were not necessary.

By using her name, Suminda was able to focus and know that the communication was for her; backing up verbal instruction with simple signs she was able to interpret the cues given and regained confidence to go with the play leader.

67

Consider how you are communicating and what the play environment is communicating. It is too confusing for the child? To enhance the play experience for Suminda, the play environment needs to have less sensory experiences in order to reduce overload. Introduce new activities and ideas one at a time. Let the child have time to assimilate new information and experiment with play. By introducing her to activities one by one, Suminda will be enabled to participate, rather than being disabled by having too much choice and stimulation, which she is unable to process and cope with. All it takes is a little forethought and planning.

Play workers need to recognise their own impact on the play space. Be aware of how children with autism respond to adults and other children. It may be difficult to understand when you are being invited to play by the child. The invitation may be obscure and have no social context. Try not to take over the child's play and tell the child how to play and what to do. Instead, be patient, helping the child to participate by offering play opportunities, but not taking over.

 **Joe's play setting had decided to make models of red fire engines. The table was set up with red paint, boxes and various loose parts for the children to use.**

When Joe saw the red materials, he was excited. "I want to make a tomato," he said. "No, not today, we are making fire engines," responded the play worker.

Joe was very disappointed and did not take part in the activity.

The play worker had not enhanced Joe's play experience. Instead of encouraging imagination, she had vetoed Joe's own idea and consequently excluded him from the activity. We need to support children to participate fully. Why not make a tomato?

So far, we have not mentioned other children. The play worker needs to encourage social interaction to increase the benefits of play and help all children to learn social interaction and communication skills. Many children on the spectrum will need encouragement to join in activities. Look for opportunities where children can play together where both parties enjoy the activity.

Remember, children are individuals first. Just because a child happens to have autism they may not wish to be friends with another child on the spectrum. Look for children's likes and interests and what they enjoy doing. Encourage friendships based on these similarities and not on a diagnosed condition.

Adaptations made to ensure the inclusion of the child on the autism spectrum must not be detrimental to other children's play experiences. If the child on the spectrum interrupts others' play, then he or she must understand the boundaries and acceptable behaviour within the play setting.

Offer assisted play as appropriate, but remember that play should be freely chosen by the child. Act as an enabler to play rather than taking over. Remember, children on the autism spectrum may have a lack of organised thought. You may need to 'structure' play on their behalf.

During play, try to reduce the amount of repeated task failure; otherwise, this may lead to frustration and a lack of motivation. If the child does not feel that they are achieving their aim, and does not enjoy the activity, they will not wish to repeat it, and the experience will put them off trying out new activities in the future.

We also need to consider siblings. Often, these children do not have the same play opportunities as other children. Their play is limited because it is difficult for parents to take the family out or invite friends round. Within play settings, siblings can be called upon to support staff working with the child on the spectrum.

Nyasha is Suminda's sister; she attends the same play scheme and tries to play with her own friends. However, Nyasha feels a sense of responsibility for Suminda and constantly looks over to see how she is getting on.

Staff do not always understand Suminda's communication, so they call Nyasha to help interpret for them. If Suminda gets upset, Nyasha is asked to help calm her down. At home, Mum will say: "Let me know if Suminda needs me. I'm just going to hang out the washing" or: "Let Suminda sit in the front seat of the car; otherwise she will scream." Nyasha's life and play experience is interrupted constantly; she is not given the freedom to play freely.

Be aware of the unintentional responsibilities given to siblings. Remember **siblings of children on the autism spectrum need to play too!**

Chapter Six:
Ideas for play

Let's go back to the challenge: how can you create a range of play opportunities that enable children and young people to extend their play when their specific interest is in *Thomas the Tank Engine*?

Remember, these ideas are just the beginning. Let them fire your imagination and encourage you to try new things with the children you are working with.

**Challenge 1:
Sensory play using sand**

Ideas:

- Tell a story of Thomas being trapped in the sand. Take a Thomas model outside and bury him in the sandpit. The only way he can be unburied is if the child participates in the story. Perhaps Thomas is the rescuer and digs out another character that is trapped. Use Thomas to pull trucks of sand from one place to another.

- Spread sand out on a flat surface. Use Thomas to create sand tracks by running him over the spread sand. Use your finger to create tracks in the sand and run Thomas along these tracks. Expand this activity by spreading out a thin layer of sand and encourage the child to draw in the sand with their finger. Expand this activity and play a game of noughts and crosses in the sand. When you have done this, shake the tray and start again. Consider using pictures of Thomas and another character to represent the noughts and crosses, still playing in the sand.

- Draw simple line drawings on to paper. Try pouring sand from a small container following the lines of the drawing to create pictures out of sand. Expand this idea and take a bucket of sand outside. What about creating a giant sand picture of Thomas the Train?

- Mix sand with blue paint, and paint pictures of Thomas, creating a textured surface that can be touched when dried, thereby encouraging sensory activities. Use the train wheels to print with.
- Put some sand into a container and shake to represent the sound of Thomas travelling on the railway lines. Use the shaker to make sounds to play against the theme tune. Consider other sounds that appear within Thomas stories. Expand the activity by taking the child around the play setting to find loose parts that sound like aspects of the story.
- Use the sand to make scenery for Thomas, such as hills and valleys. Extend this play by using natural materials such as twigs, stones, rocks and water.
- Create shapes associated with Thomas out of double-sided tape (round face, rectangular body). Stick on to paper or card. Peel the backing paper away and dip the paper into sand. The sand will stick to the uncovered double-sided tape. Create sand pictures of Thomas. This activity may require too much imagination for some children. If so, then paint glue over the top of a Thomas picture and dip into sand.
- Pour some sand outside on to a hard surface. Create a human Thomas train and take the children on a sensory journey in bare feet. Get them to walk over grass, perhaps in water, on to sand, material and plastic sheeting. Use the interest in Thomas to expand the types of play that can be experienced.
- Tell a story of Thomas involving time. Consider making a simple timer using sand that runs through one container to another via a very small hole. This works well with two see-through yogurt pots. Add sand to one; make a very small hole in a piece of card and glue it over the top of the pot. Glue the other pot to the other side of the card and you have your own simple timer.
- Try putting Thomas on an incline and adding sand to his truck until he begins to run down the slope.
- Think about how to use sand to weigh other items. Make a simple pair of scales using two containers fixed by string to a stick. Find the central balance point and balance over the back of chair or other beam. Put a Thomas model in one side and see how much sand needs to be put in the other side to balance. Expand this idea and repeat with different items to weigh

Once the child is used to playing with sand, encourage sand play without Thomas being there.

Ideas:

- Many Thomas stories involve sharing. Pick a story that is familiar to the child and try to act it out using characters. Expand the activity so that you and the child become characters in the story. Consider using face masks, badges or cardboard costumes. Encourage other children to join in.

- Use Thomas pictures to develop card games that involve sharing in a similar fashion to Happy Families.

- Use the familiar theme tune and help the child develop actions for each of the characters. Involve other children. Create an action song based on the ideas from the children. Think about movement songs such as 'Head, shoulders, knees and toes' based on the steam train, i.e. funnel, tender, footplate.

- Create a Thomas train with carriages, using cardboard boxes. Encourage children to decorate their own boxes. Remember that for some children this is too imaginative. Have some pictures of Thomas and his friends available to cut up and paste on to the boxes. Encourage the children to work together to set up the completed train. If the train is large enough, encourage the children to use their imagination and get in the train for a journey. Where is the train going? What is the story? The child who has an interest in Thomas the Tank Engine may feel able to contribute and, by being given an opportunity to use his interest, will increase his self-esteem and confidence.

- Work with a group of children to bake cakes, sharing ingredients and equipment. Allow the children to decorate individually. Focus on Thomas for the child who has the particular interest. For some children, you will need to provide examples prior to baking so that the child knows what they are aiming for. Remember, the experiences of handling the flour and mixing are just as important as the finished product. Allow children to experiment with sensory activities.

- Adapt games such as Snakes and Ladders. Use Thomas as a counter; the ladders become train tracks for Thomas to follow. Play with a group of children. Help children on the spectrum to understand waiting and turn taking, social interaction and communication.

- Work together with a group of children using modelling clay to create characters. The child obsessed with Thomas may choose to make a train. Discuss the characters and encourage children to make up a story based on them. To extend this idea take photographs of the characters and create a short story book, or make short films of the characters with all children working together in a group.
- Expand this idea further by introducing a range of loose parts and asking the children to think about what they could be and how to incorporate them into the story. For example, we previously used an image of a large cotton cone as a loose part. What could this be? Perhaps a mountain that the train needs to climb or a trunk of a tree?

 Challenge 3:
Activities that encourage imagination

Ideas:
- Consider the colours of the characters in the stories. How can they be used to create imaginative play? Use paint, modelling clay, building blocks, coloured sand/rice/pasta, card and paper. Find out what else the child may enjoy and make character coloured objects, for instance, a 'blue dog Thomas'.
- Use pictures of special interests, glue to card, cut up and make your own jigsaws.
- Consider creating puppets of characters and encourage the child to make up their own stories. There are many types of puppets: stick, string, finger, hand and glove.
- For higher functioning children on the spectrum gather a range of items that make sounds using things around you and other loose parts. Print a number of single words or short sentences. Support the child to develop a story based around familiar words and themes, using the sounds to illustrate the story. Support the child to present their 'audio play' to others.
- Create a Thomas feely book. Look for representational materials that can be incorporated, for instance, use bubble wrap to represent smoke and steam, shiny paper to represent water, and ribbon to represent tracks. If the child is finding this difficult, stick the items over an existing picture of Thomas so the representation becomes tangible for the child to see.

Encourage the use of **non-representational materials**, for instance, boxes with no lids, pieces of cloth, ribbons, string, modelling clay, balloons, sticks, bubbles, and water to encourage imagination and tactile stimulation.

The previous ideas were based around a specific interest. You could adapt these to encourage greater play experiences for children who are obsessed with dinosaurs, fairies, stars and planets, animals, farming, fishing, trees, boats, lights and clocks. The list is endless, and the challenge is to broaden the child's horizons and your own thinking.

We have recognised that children on the spectrum lack imagination and often think in a very literal sense. Some ideas may seem alien to them. Be aware of the individual child, explain your ideas and leave space for the child to consider, think and plan for themselves. Be there to enable play, rather than take over.

Play does not have to conform to the toy manufacturers' intentions. We do not have to spend lots of money in purchasing toys for our children. There is still fun to be had from a cardboard box, some paint and glue. Our role is to encourage creative thinking and allow children to use their own imagination. Some children on the spectrum may just need a little more encouragement.

Don't forget the value of dens and hiding places. All children enjoy having secret places where they can make play spaces. Encourage children on the spectrum to participate in creating spaces to play.

The following ideas are known to be favourites for children on the autism spectrum as they involve repetition, continuity and control. These are only a few suggestions. What else can you think of?

Visual stimuli

- Bubbles (remember Christopher's story). Think about how bubbles can be used to enhance sensory play
- Shape/colour matching
- Sorting toys
- Jigsaws (consider getting the children to make their own)
- Jack-in-the-box and other puppets
- Lego/construction toys
- Discovery or interactive books with flaps and features (consider getting the children to make their own)

- Make and fly kites, paper aeroplanes, windmills
- Playing with ribbons in the breeze or attached to a fan
- Play with water, particularly pouring water, adding visual stimuli to bottles of water such as glitter and beads
- Play with reflections, mirrors and torches
- Making cartoon flip books that show the same cartoon each time they are used

Physical activities

- Repetitive activities that involve movement such as action songs
- Catching balls, table tennis, swing ball
- Soft play/sensory equipment (can be made easily and cheaply)
- Slides, swings and static equipment that requires repetition
- Sandpits and diggers, buckets and spades
- Trampolines
- Sliding along wet plastic sheeting covered with washing up liquid!
- Massage or stroking skin with a feather, blowing on to skin, stroking hair
- The same physical play over and over again such as being swung in the air, rolling down slopes, jumping over a rope, skipping
- Running and climbing
- Stroking an animal over and over
- Marble runs

Social activities

Children on the autism spectrum may find socialising very difficult. Social activities work well if there is a common interest such as the local narrow gauge railway club, a camera club or a chess club. As adults we congregate together and form friendships based on common interests. Consider what the children enjoy and look at forming social activities around these areas:

- Singing/dancing especially Karaoke
- Storytelling or book clubs based around interests
- Picture lotto, Snap, Snakes and Ladders, Ludo, chess, and repetitive activities that have clear rules and boundaries
- Group activities with a purpose and end result such as creating models from Lego in groups, baking, play acting (depends on individual child)
- Swimming or playing in or with water
- Games which involve order and sequence that are shared within a group

Catherine wants to socialise but finds it difficult to build and sustain relationships. Her local autism group run an evening social group called 'Wanted Art'.

Each week the children and young people attending bring along something to do that is artistic. It may be modelling, painting, photographic or drawing cartoons on the computer. The group allows freedom of activity but is semi structured, based around art.

The activities are provided to give the young people a chance to socialise, meet each other and build friendships. Catherine says: "This is the first time I have met other people who think like me. I like it here. I can come without my mum and if I want to make a cup of tea it's okay; I don't need to ask, and if I get it wrong it does not matter."

The group has been going for several years, providing an opportunity for young people with Aspergers Syndrome to socialise and build relationships. The young people have an opportunity to go out to concerts and the cinema. Confidence has grown and, with support, many of the young people have moved on to build their own external friendships using some of the skills learned through Wanted Art.

Summary

We began by looking at the barriers to play faced by children on the autism spectrum and considered the barriers from the parents' and play providers' perspective. The book has taken us on a journey, identifying what these barriers mean in reality through the use of case studies and short stories following the triad of impairment.

There have been many insights into the world of autism, providing food for thought. The next stage is for you to take this forward and to start thinking 'outside the box', to enable children on the autism spectrum to play.

It is not just about the types of activities that are offered to children; it is broader than that. Inclusion is around understanding, accommodating and adapting, ensuring all opportunities are equally accessible to all children and young people.

No one gets it right all the time. An idea or strategy may work well the first time, but may not achieve the same result again. Be patient, take time to listen, take time to watch and observe and get to know the children. Be aware of how children present within the triad and what you might need to do to ensure they are included.

Remember, communication is a key to ensuring children are included. Be prepared to do some research around the type of communication systems children use, and remember to communicate with others, including parents.

The most important thing to remember is that the child is a child first, who just happens to have an autism spectrum condition. Don't let the autism come before the child.

Persevere. It really is worth supporting and watching for that magic moment of true engagement!

Chapter Seven: Further information

The Play Doctors
Publish adults' and children's books, practical resources and training.
www.theplaydoctors.co.uk
Tel: + 44 (0)1234 757768
Email: info@theplaydoctors.co.uk

The National Autistic Society
Support, advice and information on autism spectrum conditions.
http://www.autism.org.uk
The National Autistic Society, 393 City Road, London EC1V 1NG
Tel: +44 (0)20 7833 2299
Fax: +44 (0)20 7833 9666
Email: nas@nas.org.uk

OAASIS
Offers Advice, Assistance, Support and Information on Special needs.
http://www.oaasis.co.uk
Oaasis, The Croft , Vicars Hill, Boldre, Lymington, Hants SO41 5QB **Tel:**
+44 (0)800 197 3907
Email: oaasis@cambiangroup.com

Mencap
www.mencap.org.uk
Supporting learning disabilities.
England Mencap Office, 123 Golden Lane, London EC1Y 0RT
Tel: + 44 (0)20 7454 0454
Fax: + 44 (0)20 7608 3254
Email: mailto:information@mencap.org.uk

KIDS Charity for Disabled Children
www.kids.org.uk
Providing direct work with children, support for parents, publications and training.
KIDS, 6 Aztec Row, Berners Road, London N1 0PW
Tel: + 44 (0)20 7359 3073

The Disabilities Trust
www.autism-awareness.org.uk
First Floor, Market Place, Burgess Hill, West Sussex RH15 9NP
Tel: + 44 (0)1444 239123
Fax: + 44 (0)1444 244978
Email: info@disabilities-trust.org.uk

The Council for Disabled Children
http://www.ncb.org.uk/cdc/home.aspx
Council for Disabled Children, NCB, 8 Wakley Street, London EC1V 7QE
Tel: + 44(0)20 7843 1900
Fax: + 44 (0)20 7843 6313
Email: cdc@ncb.org.uk

Autism Resources
Access to many resources to support autism through this site.
www.autism-resources.com

Inside the bubble
Free autism resources for home use and not for profit organisations.
www.insidethebubble.co.uk

About the author:
Wendy Usher has worked with children and young people for more than 30 years. She has managed various children's organisations and has been teaching adults for twenty years. Wendy started her business, The Play Doctors, in 2007 to concentrate on supporting inclusion. Wendy is married with two grown-up children and two grandchildren.

Other practical resource books include:

The Play Doctors also publish a range of children's books based on a group of animal friends. The characters have a range of impairments, and the stories identify how they adapt their games and adventures to ensure all the friends can participate. These children's stories have an accompanying adults' resource book full of ideas for creative play and activities.

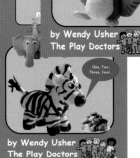

For further information about these and associated training courses please contact

The Play Doctors on:
01234 757768
email: info@theplaydoctors.co.uk
or www.theplaydoctors.co.uk

All rights reserved. No part of this publication may be reproduced, stored in retrieval system, or transmitted in any form or by any means electronic, mechanical, photocopying or recording.
Author Wendy Usher   © **The Play Doctors 2011**

The Play Doctors Publishing Company is a trading arm of The Play Doctors Ltd. ®

Reg Office: The Play Doctors, 13 Bourne End, Cranfield, Bedfordshire MK43 0AX